Wisdom to Recover By

STUDY TOPICS FOR
People Growing in Sobriety

CECIL C.

CompCare Publishers
2415 Annapolis Lane
Minneapolis, Minnesota 55441

© 1990 Cecil C.
All rights reserved.
Published in the United States
by CompCare Publishers.

Reproduction in whole or part, in any form, including storage in memory device system, is forbidden without written permission... except that portions may be used in broadcast or printed commentary or review when attributed fully to author and publication by names.

C., Cecil
  Wisdom to recover by — study topics for people growing in sobriety
Cecil C.
  p.cm.
  ISBN 0-89638-203-6
  1. Alcoholics—Rehabilitation. 2. Alcoholism—Psychological aspects. I. Title.
HV5275.C15 1990   90-1642
362.29'286—dc20   CIP

Cover design by Susan Rinek

Inquiries, orders, and catalog requests should be addressed to
CompCare Publishers
2415 Annapolis Lane
Minneapolis, Minnesota 55441
Call toll free 800/328-3330
(Minnesota residents 612/559-4800)

5	4	3	2	1
94	93	92	91	90

To my daughters
Gwen and Lori

Contents

Introduction	1
The Need for Pain	5
Who Is an Alcoholic?	9
The Need to Change	15
Hitting Bottom	19
Acceptance	23
A Higher Power	27
Spiritual, Not Religious	31
The Role of Honesty	35
Denial	39
People-Pleasing	43
Rationalizing	47
Self-Pity	51
Resentments	55
Anger	59
Fear	63
Hostility	67
The Gift of Humility	71
Becoming Grateful	75
Our Insanities	79
Stinkin' Thinkin'	83
What Sobriety Takes Away	87
Willingness	91
Our Obsession	95
The Dry Drunk	99
Why Slips Happen	103
Loneliness	107
Spiritual Living	113

Use of Prayer 117
The Sense of Belonging 121
It's a Simple Program 125
People Who Need People 129
Love 133

Introduction

Regardless of how old or "intellectual" we are when we attain a comfortable state of sobriety, our sobriety must be sustained.

To sustain recovery and grow spiritually, we must continue adding to our knowledge of living—living without an addictive substance, living without compulsive behavior, living without obsessiveness. Recovery from alcoholism is an ongoing process that involves learning, change, and growth; essentially, recovery puts us back in school again and again.

In the world of recovery, there are many stories of men and women who successfully stopped drinking, then gradually became complacent. A closer look reveals that these recovering alcoholics became complacent when they stopped participating in mutual-help sessions, stopped reading recovery literature, and stopped attending helpful lectures and other presentations. In time, these recovering alcoholics began to slip back into the agony and despair of alcoholism, an addiction they thought they'd left behind forever.

One simple adage seems to be consistently true for the recovering alcoholic: *when the pupil is ready, the teacher will appear.* And because "teachers" come into our lives through information that we read and hear, it is essential that we remain open to many sources of wisdom that help us learn, change, and grow. When we fail to attend Twelve Step meetings, we miss valuable opportunities to gain new information and insights that may be vital to sustaining recovery.

Many of us in Alcoholics Anonymous have had the following experience: In the course of working the program, we encounter the same words, phrases, and concepts many times without having much reaction to them. But then, at certain times, this familiar information seems to speak directly to us—we are struck by its relevance to our recovery. Suddenly, it seems, we are ready to integrate this information into our lives.

Whether we gain new information through hearing something or reading something, we all can find something brand new and helpful in something familiar and/or old. This is why oldtimers in the Program advise newcomers about the "meetings...meetings...meetings" they might expect and advise them not to allow dust to gather on the "Big Book." These *teachers* of ours often say that "There are no 'same old things' for those who need to learn."

An ancient proverb tells us that when we find a teacher, we find a friend. The things we read and hear and the people we share thoughts with could be considered new, friendly teachers. When we continue on in our recovery as seekers, even ancient wisdom and things we've heard a thousand times can be as fresh as today's dawn.

We grow spiritually through revelations—revelations about ourselves, our disease of alcoholism, and our capabilities and limitations. Early in our recovery, most of us are given a powerful, if somewhat cryptic, message: that *we alone* have the power to make our lives purposeful and free of addictive substances, but that *alone* we cannot do it.

In recovery, we develop a new dependency—a beautiful and vital dependency—on people who share in the principles of our recovery program. We are people who need people, most particularly others who are recovering. Their support, love, and advice help us survive and sustain our recovery as well. There is no question that we need the advice of others who have come before us; we gain strength through the ideas and experiences of others. Knowledge is perhaps the most important agent of change. Words we read and words we hear inspire us to change and help us with the process. We need to continue learning about the tools for spiritual growth. But awareness is not enough. Growth and change cannot be forced upon us, nor can growth and change fall softly on our shoulders like a spring rain. *We must be active participants in our own change and growth.*

We learn that we cannot change *anyone*. Nor can anyone change *us*. Even our recovery process, with all its guiding principles, cannot revamp us. *The process of recovery can only give us the appropriate tools with which to change ourselves.* Other people can help by showing us how they learned, through challenge and heartache, to effectively use the tools made available to us through our Program. But other people cannot do it *for* us.

Alcoholics Anonymous does make promises in return for sobriety. Magnificent promises. But the paragraph describing the positive changes we can expect in sobriety goes on to state that these changes will materialize only "...if we work for them."

Of course, altered attitudes, changes in character, and spiritual growth require considerable input about where we've been in terms of our alcoholism and where we're going in our recovery. In sustaining our recovery, we learn to appreciate attending a school from which there is no graduation. This being true, the author will feel rewarded if readers derive from the short essays in this book some help in remaining serenely and securely sober. It is hoped, also, that these essays might provide some inspiration for group discussion.

■ ■ ■

The Need for Pain

It could be said that as free people, we have the inalienable right to hurt ourselves as much as we wish.

Everyone, from time to time, engages in self-defeating behavior that results in pain. Alcoholics compulsively engage in self-defeating behavior that they *know* will result in pain—and they do so time and time again. The alcoholic's dependency is driven by a compulsion that must be satisfied mentally, emotionally, and physically. Most of us recovering alcoholics will confess that we once held the belief that *"anything worth doing is worth doing to excess."*

But the very real pain that a drinking alcoholic experiences actually can prove to be a blessing. Consider this: if alcohol could consistently perpetuate the state of euphoria experienced during the first stage of intoxication, few drunks ever would have a desire or need to stop drinking.

Abuse of alcohol brings pain to all areas of an alcoholic's life. Many of us were motivated to cry out for release from this pain. But, then, we saw no convincing reason to stop using this drug—as long as we could afford to buy "relief" in the form of alcohol or other drugs, and as long as we could count on being "rescued" by others from the consequences of our behavior.

We recovering alcoholics invariably consider our past pain and wonder why we had to suffer so much before we accepted the fact that we simply *cannot drink*. Through our own experiences, many of us finally came to understand the observation that "some people have to be crushed by a falling brick wall before they are impressed."

Many philosophers have stressed the force of pain in changing lives. Out of suffering comes a clearer understanding of values; pain spurs growth. Some spiritual leaders identify pain as the starting point for progress toward the fulfillment of life. Indeed, the teachings of Buddha focus to a large extent on suffering. Five hundred years before Christ, Buddha preached that the First Noble Truth is that happiness is the result of getting free from suffering.

When Christ began his Sermon on the Mount, he gave his followers the Eight Beatitudes, the first being this: *"Blessed are the poor in spirit, for theirs is the Kingdom of Heaven."* Some theologians interpret this to mean that regenerative wisdom begins with deflation of the ego.

Many people say that the success of Alcoholics Anonymous is rooted in the axiom that all spiritual experiences have universal common denominators—pain, suffering, calamity, helplessness, and a deflation of the ego. Indeed, painful degradation readies people to grasp any helping hand that might lift them out of their agony.

The First Step of Alcoholics Anonymous parallels both the First Noble Truth and the First Beatitude in that it refers to a spiritual experience that results from suffering: *"We admitted we were powerless over alcohol—that our lives had become unmanageable."*

Most authorities on the disease of alcoholism agree that so long as people in the life of the alcoholic prevent the alcoholic from confronting the consequences of his or her behavior, intoxication will remain a curiously attractive and positive experience in the mind of the drinker. Families and friends of alcoholics are often advised that permitting the alcoholic to drink *and to suffer the conse-*

quences is a more effective way to guide the alcoholic toward help than accepting his or her apologies and most fervent promises to never get drunk again.

One important activity in the treatment of alcoholism is directed toward awakening so-called enablers or codependents of the alcoholic to an important fact: that rescuing a person from the consequences of his or her drinking behavior may actually prolong that person's alcoholism by ten years or more.

Pain was our beginning; pain finally drove us to seek answers; pain made us humbly ask for help. Feeling the pain and finally surrendering to it motivated us to seek the highest of human attainments—to live a more spiritual, balanced, and loving life.

■　■　■

Who Is an Alcoholic?

Many people use the word *alcoholic* as an adjective rather than a noun. In fact, this particular word seems to be used somewhat freely to describe one of a number of things: a state of weakness, lack of character, uselessness, hopelessness, and immorality. As an adjective, the word is often used to characterize the mind of someone who gets drunk too often and stays "blotto" too long.

"She's an alcoholic failure" or "He's an alcoholic coward" are considered perfect descriptive appraisals by some. And the list of words used to characterize alcoholism is long and varied—from "weakling" to "bully"; from "slob" to "bore."

Those familiar with the disease of alcoholism have a sad but true response to nonaddicted social drinkers who denounce alcoholics for "bringing disgrace on themselves" and being "solely to blame" for perpetuating their own problems. Indeed, anyone who drinks alcohol might be told the following: *There but for the grace of God go you.*

Even in today's relatively enlightened society, a person struggling with alcohol dependency might freely admit to being a problem drinker, yet cringe at the thought of being labeled an alcoholic. Since everyone has "troubles," the drinker finds some solace and face-saving in the gentle designation of "problem drinker." While people may willingly acknowledge that they have some problems with alcohol, they perceive alcoholics as *losers*. But partial, grudging admission of a serious problem and a need for help deters the process of recovery.

Research has generally failed to conclude that there are specific personality traits responsible for projecting a social drinker into chronic alcoholism. But there is general agreement that certain characteristics are quite common in people who are addicted to alcohol.

Among researchers who probe the causes of alcoholism are some who advance the Personality Trait Theory. While these researchers concede that alcoholics do not necessarily share the same personality characteristics, they do report evidence that in prealcoholism stages, certain personality patterns seem to suggest predisposition toward addiction.

We alcoholics seem unable to profit from experience. We may convincingly moan that we've learned our lesson; we proclaim that we'll never binge again, then we subsequently return with great eagerness to what we know will bring us agonizing pain.

The Second Step implies that we have lost our sanity. How insane are we? Well, we'd never stick a finger in a light socket again if we got a jolt that knocked us flat. We alcoholics probably learned the lesson about electricity, but we didn't grasp a similar lesson about drinking.

Generally, characteristics common to the alcoholic are said to be: egocentricity, low tolerance for stress, dependence, and a sense of omnipotence. Add to these characteristics a deep sense of inadequacy, persistent fear of rejection, and shattering insecurity.

We alcoholics tend to sense rejection even when there is none. We are also blind to, or we minimize, *genuine* acceptance by others. When offers of friendship are most obvious, we distrust the signs and the motivations.

We alcoholics equate sensitivity with lack of self-confidence. Furthermore, real defeat and rejection overwhelm us with a sense of unworthiness. "I just can't win," we may sob. Yet there is one place where we erroneously believe we can find total acceptance and escape from "injustices"—deep down in a bottle.

Hostility is almost sure to be present in the alcoholic. Chronic rage may be manifested during spells of sobriety or it may lie dormant until we are drunk, hallucinating, or dreaming— then it flares.

Unfortunately, an urge for self-destruction is present in many alcoholics. Low self-esteem teams with chronic anger to the extent that many alcoholics seriously consider ending their lives.

Our emotional immaturity creates in us a dependency on others for the basics of life and for bailing us out of trouble.

We alcoholics are also likely to have a low tolerance for delays and deterrants. We want all good things—and we want them *now*. Unrealistically high expectations and aspirations accompanied by lack of control seem to provide a recipe for failure in our lives. Disappointment nurtures resentments and these resentments develop into depression. In the mind of the addicted drinker, alcohol is the only real solution for problems.

All alcoholics experience, to some degree, two emotional merry-go-rounds. One merry-go-round is denial. Over and over, around and around, we find excuses for our compulsive drinking. The second merry-go-round is the unending search for relief from pain brought on by disturbed feelings, thoughts, and sensations. Alcohol is a depressant; at first it soothes. But once the soothing effect of alcohol wears off, the mental anguish returns, stronger than before. This pain seems to require more "medicine." Anesthetized emotions are followed by more pain. Then, a return to the temporary comfort of drugs. Around and around goes the cycle until the merry-go-round comes to an inevitable halt—with severe psychological, emotional, and physical problems, perhaps even death.

In some cases, practicing alcoholics may be the most difficult patients to diagnose. If hospitalized, we yell so loudly for release that we are likely to be set free. Then, at home, we invariably call out for help when our agony is most acute. Those "times" are probably at two, three, or four o'clock in the morning, when the after-effects of a binge are most disturbing. Little wonder that we run the risk of being categorized as neurotic nuisances by family, friends, and perhaps even medical professionals.

It is a fallacy that the personality of the alcoholic, by definition, includes a weak will. In reality, we alcoholics have astoundingly strong will power. How else but by grim determination could we "come to" with a devastating hangover on the morning of a work day, gulp three or four "slugs" before one stays down, then drive or ride to work and hang on throughout the day with surprising displays of efficiency?

The vast majority of us were "functioning drinkers." For a period of time—perhaps years—many of us kept our addiction hidden from bosses, coworkers, friends, and perhaps even family members. Ultimately, the bottom fell out, yet many of the people in our lives were surprised to learn that we had any problems with alcohol at all.

Some say there are two kinds of alcoholics—male and female. Others say there are two kinds of alcoholics—drunk and sober. Actually, there *are* two kinds of alcoholics—daily drinkers and periodics, those who stay on the wagon for days or weeks, then go on a binge. But despite the surface differences between these two kinds of alcoholics, they are really very much the same. *We alcoholics succumb to that first drink, no matter when or why we take it.*

Both the troubled social drinker and the alcoholic may be helped by consulting with a mental health professional. For the alcoholic, however, one form of therapy is absolutely essential—abstinence.

The Need to Change

When we begin striving to achieve sobriety, many of us evidence split personalities: as we cry out for relief from the pain of our addiction, we continue to insist that we have no intention of giving up our trusted friend, alcohol. Perhaps the suffering alcoholic is the greatest adherent to the belief that one can have his or her cake and eat it, too.

But before we can learn how to live with total abstinence, we need to change our attitude. This need for change applies not only for us drinkers, but for all others who are close to us— spouses, parents, children, friends, associates, and employers.

It was difficult for us and for many of our loved ones to realize a rather basic rule of life: that all people are in the process of change at all times, whether or not they're aware of it. The struggle to cope with the challenges of life makes change imperative. Without forward movement, regression takes control. Positive people show progress. Negative people, the passive ones, decline progress by giving up.

For alcoholics and their families, perhaps the saddest, most dangerous words are these: *"What's the use?"* It is the rare alcoholic who is truly hopeless. Just short of the grave or an institution, a drinker can change his or her attitude. But only the alcoholic can make the decision to change; other people can serve merely as guides to an objective.

Love and understanding are the most helpful things other people can give a troubled drinker. It sometimes comes as a revelation to those close to an alcoholic that while they cannot *do* anything to aid the drinker, they can *be* things that he or she can see and draw inspiration and encouragement from. Many alcoholics have found the motivation to seek sobriety only when the people in their lives stopped trying to change them and instead simply changed their own reactions to the alcoholic's behavior.

Near-miracles can occur when family members and friends make the following changes: from negative thinking to positive thinking, from contempt for the drinker's actions to respect for the drinker's potential, from fear and apprehension to faith and hope, from rejection to acceptance.

It was more difficult for us to refuse to do anything about our drinking when the attitudes of those around us moved from dominance to encouragement, from panic to serenity, from false to real hope, and particularly from driving hands to guiding hands.

Our years of addiction to alcohol made most of us rebellious, arrogant troublemakers. It is not easy for such persons to make changes vital to a sober existence. Recovery seldom is an immediate success. We will have this incurable but arrestable disease all the days of our lives.

To make the change from active alcoholics to sober citizens, we had to make painful efforts to accomplish difficult things. Oftentimes, our attempts to maintain sobriety were the sole result of need and desire nurtured by dire necessity.

Staying sober, in even moderate contentment, required that we give up more than just alcohol. Old ideas and modes of behavior had to be acknowledged and eliminated from our lives. We had to go all the way in our efforts to change from the "old us." Half-measures, we learned, invariably led to compromise. We not only accepted the fact that we have a disease, we also applied ourselves to new attitudes and directions that led to change and recovery.

Unless we are vigilant in holding on to our changed ideas about alcohol and drinking, we may too easily find reasons for again turning to that "one little drink" that will turn into "one big drunk."

Hitting Bottom

The "bottom" is the point at which we are ready to surrender to reality, to admit our addiction, and to accept the fact that we need help because we cannot sober up alone.

It has been said that "You hit bottom when you stop digging." This is the point when we stop denying, stop making alibis and excuses, and stop looking for loopholes.

Some people assume that hitting bottom necessarily means that we must lose everything and end up on skid row before we're ready to start our journey back to sobriety. This, of course, is untrue. Actually, it has been estimated that only about three percent of the alcoholics in this country are living on skid row.

Each alcoholic has his or her own "bottom"—it is that person's discovery of humility, the surrender required to admit a deep personal failure and a corresponding need for help. But every alcoholic fights the acknowledgment that he or she is completely defeated.

Those of us who have "been there and back" know that the bottom is not really physical, no matter how miserable the physical suffering. It seems that no crisis or personal catastrophe is ever potent enough to bring surrender. We had to discover on a spiritual level that we were defeated and could no longer fight with our own power.

The "miracle" of Alcoholics Anonymous is characterized as the vital act of surrender needed for the drinker to reach for help, plus the fellowship that fills the resulting void—the constant contact with men and women who have lived through addiction and recovery.

For many of us, hitting bottom is the necessary mastering the ego that insists on the right to drink by saying: "It's my own life I'm gambling with. I'm not hurting anyone else. I'm not that bad off. When I'm good and ready, I'll quit. I can do it, too."

The unconquerable ego that bitterly opposes any notion of defeat lies within everyone. It can make so many things possible—both good and bad. In the case of the alcoholic, there is no hope for a step toward recovery until this unconquerable ego is reduced or rendered ineffective. Bill W., cofounder of Alcoholics Anonymous, once described surrender in a letter to Dr. Carl Jung as "ego collapse in depth."

American philosopher William James wrote that "the crisis of self-surrender is throwing ourselves on the mercy of powers which, whatever they may be, are more ideal than ours." Basically, this is asking for help to combat that which is beating us to an emotional pulp. Some ask, "Isn't surrender a weakness?" The answer can be, "*Everyone* has weaknesses— including pride, which has been called the greatest weakness of all." The rigidity of the ego can be a destructive weakness indeed.

Recovering alcoholics often say this with a chuckle: "I finally was cut down to size. Fortunately, I got the message." We know that the battle against our disease is one in which *surrender* brings victory. We realize we had two choices, both of which involved defeat and surrender: giving in to a need for help, or succumbing to the disease of alcoholism. Below all other "bottoms" is the descent to prison or the grave.

Recovering alcoholics are familiar with the sensation of living on a blissful pink cloud. This is the logical aftermath when ego is deflated. In recovery, we are cautioned not to relax our guard. We are told never to think of an ego as being dead and buried. A suppressed ego has an astounding capacity for rebirth and its return can precipitate a quick fall off a pink cloud.

Wise recovering alcoholics know that staying sober may be simple, but not easy. These folks continually remind themselves that "I stopped being headstrong. I can't go back to that habit again."

We may enjoy cloud nine, but we need this reminder: "Just be a sober person, not an angel."

Acceptance

When the physical torment of alcoholism is eased through abstinence, emotional recovery can begin.

When we abstain from drinking, we stay "well" with a level of comfort that some consider a miracle. But we cannot depend on miracles in the process of maintaining our sobriety. Maintenance of sobriety depends on one simple condition: *that as alcoholics, we cannot regain the ability to control our use of alcohol.* Full acceptance makes us more receptive to information and help; full acceptance helps us develop a conviction about what is *vital* in our behavior. Unfortunately, some recovering people sabotage their own efforts to maintain sobriety by confusing halfhearted acceptance with full acceptance.

Anything less than full acceptance is ineffective lip-service or mere *compliance*—submission, resignation, or concession. Halfhearted acceptance is fraught with reservations and qualifications ("Maybe I'm not really an alcoholic"; "I don't see how I could be considered an alcoholic because I only drink on weekends"). This lack of certainty and clarity *will* lead eventually to the inability to accept a simple truth: that we need to stay sober.

Compliance suggests agreement without enthusiasm. As such, compliance can be a real trap for alcoholics. The compliant person's state of mind is filled with mixed feelings and divided sentiments. This kind of confused thinking leads to a willingness *with qualifications*. But passive willingness is easily crushed and willingness without action is fantasy.

Self-assurance that is only skin-deep cannot be permanent, no matter how loudly one shouts "I believe." Pain always brought us a temporary awareness of our personal problems with alcohol. While the suffering and the shakes and the sweats lasted, we didn't argue or doubt or fight the realization that alcohol was beating us down to our knees. In those cases, we readily complied with reality. After our pain eased, however, all reasons for compliance with reality disappeared. The part of our halfhearted acceptance that never really meshed with our cry for help began to grow. It took command of our thinking. The fact that we only halfheartedly accepted our drinking problems now pleased us. We blamed our pain for making us submit to advice wherever we could find it. We reneged on any promises we made to people who we now believe took advantage of our "helpless condition."

Compliance permits a "yes" to dominate the fringes of the mind while an emphatic "no" fills a drinker's insides. This inconsistency usually gives rise to a guilty conscience. The compliant person is forced to admit to himself or herself that any person who says one thing yet believes something else is untruthful. Compliant people almost always build a secret guilt in their innermost selves. Realization of their deceitful behavior leads to a sense of inferiority. Compliers know they are unreliable. They dislike themselves for not really being the kind of people they hope others think they are.

For us, compliance represented an easy way out of confrontations on the subject of our excessive drinking. Any quick offer we could make to shape up always helped us avert sticky arguments. In fact, we would promise just about *anything* because we alcoholics always want to be liked. Agreeing with others was an important part of our need to cover up. But the pretense of agreement only paved the road to sneaky, hidden drinking. We knew that if we were faced with a showdown in the near future, we would quickly deny our compliance and refuse to make good. *There is no strength in compliance.*

In admitting that we are overmatched in our personal battle with alcoholism, we accept defeat in this *one* arena. When this admission is made with a spirit of hopefulness, we fortify ourselves against disaster; failure can destroy us if we have not made our acceptance with the sincere belief that we can bounce back from a temporary relapse. *Our desire for sobriety must be a healthy urge, not a cross to bear.*

Acceptance is an antidote for self-deception because it has the effect of throwing a light on reality; acceptance helps to create a clear understanding of the *seriousness* of alcoholism. We stop fooling ourselves with alibis and rationalization. Self-deception can be fatal to the victim of *any* disease.

The easiest kind of acceptance is that which is purely intellectual. But those who seek sobriety find that acceptance on the "gut level"—in other words, emotional acceptance—is most effective for recovery. Many of us have succeeded by simplifying our acceptance to "a desire to have the desire" to stop drinking.

If we arrive at acceptance wholeheartedly, we are surrendering to reality. In recovery, we have a yardstick to determine our degree of acceptance. When acceptance brings a feeling of relaxation, even serenity, we know that we have truly surrendered. The greater the ability to truly relax in daily life, the greater the inner acceptance.

But we cannot force ourselves to "accept—or else." Acceptance must be a free and voluntary act. When there is true conviction that acceptance of reality will speed recovery, there will be progress in recovery.

Many of us who surrender to reality are pleasantly surprised by the relative ease with which we are able to be completely honest in all our affairs. Honesty comes naturally because acceptance is a positive, constructive act. Honesty enhances, rather than depletes, will power.

A positive outlook on the present and future also comes quickly after an unqualified acceptance. Happy, sober alcoholics sometimes find strength in coining phrases based on their own experiences: "I'd rather be sober by mistake than dead drunk by design," says one. Another alludes to "Having the courage of my cowardice in trying to fight booze."

We accept ourselves as we are *today*. Past horrors thankfully are gone; tomorrow's possibilities may never come. When we credit "fortunate quirks of fate" in bringing us to a program of recovery, we become humble and grateful—two character strengths necessary in sustaining sobriety and growing spiritually.

Those who genuinely accept are aware that alcoholics are a diverse lot. Even if our story is completely different from the stories of others, we find many people to identify with when we fully accept our disease. Acceptance will counteract the pattern of denial that prevented us from admitting that we have an incurable disease, just like all those other people we once believed to be so different from us.

We maintain abstinence one day at a time. But we know that "once an alcoholic, always an alcoholic." We are convinced we will die alcoholics; our goal is to die sober.

■ ■ ■

A Higher Power

When a stubbornly resisting newcomer to AA told an AA oldtimer that he wouldn't be able to completely accept the Program because he was an agnostic, the oldtimer said this to him: "You still have a choice; you can be a sober agnostic or a drunken agnostic."

This oldtimer's comment is a good summation of the Program's demands for understanding what many call "the God bit." Oldtime AA members emphasize the spiritual factor because they know from experience that spirituality is needed for ongoing recovery. Indeed, if abstinence was all that was required for a comfortable ongoing sobriety, there would be no need for anything beyond a hospital or "drying out" facility in arresting the disease of alcoholism.

With our addiction to alcohol, it seemed completely natural to us to ingest alcohol until we were drunk. Once we are abstinent, the problem is to live without the crutch provided by alcohol. This is not usually an easy accomplishment, for it means that the abstaining drunk needs to reach beyond the physical to the level that is known as spiritual.

A business owner once shared with an AA member his deep concern about the drinking behavior of two men who worked for him. Instead of firing these men, the business owner said that he hoped to help them "shake the habit." The AA member asked if the employees had tried AA. The business owner replied, "I know these men personally; I could never send them to a religious organization."

The concept of AA as a religious organization is shared by many people who are not enlightened on the subjects of alcoholism and AA. Despite the fact that people in the AA Program are encouraged to utilize prayer to find knowledge of a "Higher Power" and for guidance in dealing with their obsessions and compulsions, there are no religious formats or tenets in the AA Program.

It should be added, however, that the people who arrest the disease of alcoholism most quickly and keep it under control most effectively seem to be those people who have developed the spiritual side of their lives. Spirituality simply is the most effective way, in the long run, to cope with thoughts and actions that endanger sobriety.

Many newcomers to AA have some trouble with "the God bit." But when these newcomers adopt an attitude of listening, they place themselves in an ideal situation to obtain answers to all of their questions.

Many protesting newcomers hear this quip from oldtimers: "If God wanted man to talk more than listen, He'd have given us two mouths and only one ear."

After a period of years of ingesting alcohol, it may take several months of abstinence to restore clear thinking. Newcomers to mutual help groups frequently want to "tell it all as it is" at first. Later, they realize that too much talking can be a mistake in the earliest days of abstinence. Perhaps a good formula for participation in a mutual help group during early abstinence is 90 percent listening, 10 percent responding and asking.

It should be obvious to beginners—but it isn't always so—that in order to listen, they must keep coming back to meetings. Newcomers to AA are likely to hear this from the oldtimers in the Program: "We urge you to keep coming back so you'll see firsthand what happens to the know-it-alls who *don't* come back."

At meetings, we are encouraged to share our own "drunkalogues." Reflecting on and recounting the horrors of our incurable disease helps us continue to appreciate our sobriety. Fortunately, such stories help others to identify; everyone learns from personal stories about addiction and recovery.

Another benefit of "drunkalogues" shared in group meetings: they help make people aware of the major role that *coincidence* plays in helping a compulsive drinker make the decision to stop drinking. The number of coincidences and the stunning ways in which they befall an active alcoholic "at precisely the right time" impress most drinkers who are on the verge of getting the message. Where does that "moment of clarity" come from—that moment when we realize we must surrender and get help? Recovering alcoholics may accept these coincidences and moments of clarity as the work of a Higher Power.

Many newcomers ask how they can find a Higher Power. That Higher Power can be almost anything, including group consciousness, a concept, the power of nature, or the bond of friendship. Once we admit to ourselves and to others that there *is* a power greater than ourselves, we begin to realize that we are not running the world and that we need help.

To find faith, we need reach no more than fifteen inches. This is the distance from brain to heart.

■   ■   ■

Spiritual, Not Religious

The primary problem of the alcoholic is not the substance of alcohol, but the disease of alcoholism. The behavior, life patterns, and health status of any practicing alcoholic are determined by *what alcohol does* to his or her body and mind.

The disease of alcoholism is complicated because its progression is manifested both emotionally and physically. Recovery, dependent entirely on arresting an incurable disease, is almost never achieved without the benefit of what sober alcoholics call "the spiritual." While this spiritual factor requires faith (sometimes "blind" faith) from the drinker, this faith is not necessarily of a religious nature.

Alcoholics Anonymous expresses the nature of the spiritual aspect of the Program with the Serenity Prayer: *"God grant me the serenity to accept the things I cannot change, courage to change the things I can, and wisdom to know the difference."*

Some treatment professionals have cited the power of the Serenity Prayer as "greater than any drug known to science." Indeed, some recovering alcoholics repeat this prayer a hundred times a day as they hold on to their sobriety. One AA oldtimer wryly says, "When the tension goes way up, I may have to shout the Serenity Prayer at the top of my lungs."

The word *God*, according to AA, refers to "a power greater than ourselves." Accepting a "Higher Power" undoubtedly is the toughest decision ever made by a practicing alcoholic. We practicing alcoholics are, by nature, dishonest, stubborn egotists who refuse to accept reality and refuse to accept help.

But with the mental clarity that comes after detoxification, we readily admit that we had little power over our own behavior while we were enslaved by booze. *Alcohol was surely a power greater than ourselves.*

The chief thing that prevents us from finding "the spiritual side" is our stubborn belief that we can do it alone. We resist surrender to humility until we find out that humble people don't have to be doormats. Beginners are told that "Humility means simply that you have become open-minded and no longer are certain that you know all the answers."

It is often said that those who vehemently deny the existence of a Higher Power usually are in despair of ever finding it. Alcoholics invariably cling to reservations about a God they feel has abandoned them; many alcoholics have difficulty with blind faith.

Blind faith *should* be easy for us. When we were drinking, we certainly had blind faith in the power of alcohol to solve all our troubles. We never questioned *why* we believed in the alcohol god; we just believed.

Recovering alcoholics can give newcomers solid encouragement in understanding God: "If He were small enough to be comprehended fully, he would not be nearly great enough to fill all our needs." And on sobriety: "It's a game with only one rule. That rule is the same as the name of the game— Don't Drink!"

Prayer is vital to the spiritual side of recovery. Most of us recall that we did not look to God for help until alcohol had knocked us flat on our backs. When sober, we realize that "What we do while on our knees asking for help is not as important as the actions we take once we are back on our feet."

How to pray? In the program we hear, "Why not begin by thinking good things about someone you believe you hate?" And: "Prayer is a conversation. Try listening as well as asking." Prayer will dissolve brutal resentments. Some say, "It is hard to be angry with anyone when you are having a conversation with God."

Prayer increases our gratitude: "You cannot be resentful at the same time you are feeling grateful."

All of this may sound a little like magic. It is true that AA has a slogan that advises, "Let go and let God." This slogan is not intended to imply that sobriety can only grow in passive states of being. Instead, this slogan calls attention to the need to break through senseless and stubborn resistance to ideas. This slogan also points to the importance of banishing old resentments and negative thinking.

By throwing off self-imposed handicaps through the act of accepting unchangeable problems, the alcoholic has time to face and handle the things he or she *can* change.

None of these spiritual pursuits—accepting the help of a Higher Power of our understanding, praying to this Higher Power for guidance and strength, developing gratitude, letting go of anger and resentments—requires joining a religious organization or professing a religious belief system. The spiritual journey is completely *personal*. It requires only faith... and hard work.

In our progression through abstinence, we are reminded that the swan gliding smoothly on the surface of a lake is the very picture of serenity. But beneath the surface of the lake, the swan is working consistently and vigorously to propel itself where it wishes to go.

■ ■ ■

The Role of Honesty

It is a great relief when we finally admit that we are powerless to control our drinking. When the hidden truth in our lives is out of the closet, we feel the comfort of honesty.

We lived with self-deceit for so long that at first total honesty seemed to us like a newly discovered wonder drug. Throughout our most indiscriminate drinking, we lied about the frequency and quantity of our intake and we worked hard to cover up all evidence of untruth. Instead, we cleverly hid our supplies. When confronted with the embarrassing question, "Have you been drinking?" we'd answer, "Not really; I just had a couple."

When we gave up and were honest in asking for help with our drinking problems, we no longer felt like Atlas holding all the grief of the world on shaking shoulders and wobbly legs.

During our years of avoiding truths, we suffered intense anxiety. Not only did we fear being found out, we dreaded admitting that our defects were causing us to *fail*. Heavy ingestion of alcohol helped us lie to ourselves. By drinking our way into a stupor, we believed we could make whatever problems we had disappear. Our only weapon was to ignore something we did not have the strength to confront.

Dishonesty, of course, is a shield for everyone—the teetotaler, the social drinker, and the drunk. The difference between alcoholics and those who can control their drinking is that seemingly every physical, emotional, and mental frailty is accentuated in the alcoholic. Hence, the need for deception jolts the alcoholic far more than it does other people. This desperation factor increased the importance of tricking those around us.

We never fully realized that other people detected our dishonesty. This helped us deceive ourselves to the point that we began to believe our own lies. When we *did* acknowledge our dishonesty to ourselves, we seldom felt guilt or remorse. Instead, our warped personalities applauded our sly, crafty, clever ability to live lies. Although we admitted to ourselves that we were cheats, we developed an odd sort of pride in our ability to outwit those we considered meddlesome.

Most people who dabble in dishonesty also choose to avoid facing up to real problems. There is, for example, a tendency among such people to *worry* about something like a chest pain rather than to consult with a doctor and thereby "run the risk" of hearing something unpleasant. It is little wonder, then, that we preferred self-experimentation with "controlled" drinking to honest evaluation of our problem with someone knowledgeable about alcoholism. After all, no proud drunk wants to risk having to give up all that "pleasant" swigging of liquor.

The honesty necessary for surrendering to reality and seeking sobriety is not the "cash register" kind of honesty that, for example, prompted a young Abraham Lincoln to walk six miles in order to return six pennies to a shopkeeper who had mistakenly undercharged him.

Actually, most of us have such contempt for thievery that monetary dishonesty is our primary standard for appraising deceit. It was simple, therefore, to think of lies about our drinking as relatively unimportant or perhaps even amusing. We protested, "I'm not hurting anyone but myself." But the truth is that the injured party, in this case, is the most important person we'll ever know.

Truth is an adjunct of harmony, yet we must face the fact that unpleasantness is an integral part of truth and life. Longfellow wrote, "Into each life some rain must fall." As active alcoholics, we turned all pain, grief, fear, and frustration into self-pity rather than treating these aspects of life as essential to our existence as human beings.

Reasoning processes are adversely affected by alcohol, so it isn't surprising that we weren't very good at solving our own problems. Before we can solve our problems, we must *identify* them. But identification of truth is usually well beyond the capability of the active alcoholic.

While some may consider the simple truth bland or shallow, it is actually a *glaring reality*. And reality is recognized in various ways, depending on the individual and his or her experience. We never fully understood that a world *without* truth would be dark confusion, but that a world *with* truth is "exactly how it is."

We avoided truths because they usually were bitter. We made our own truths, all directed at others—"Those people out there are hostile; they hate me."

Truth liberated us from misery. Without truth, there can be no growth in sobriety.

■ ■ ■

Denial

Denial is one of the major symptoms of alcoholism. Denial is also one of the major obstacles to achieving sobriety.

A drinker's progression toward alcoholism will manifest a combination of many "warning signals." Of course, not all problem drinkers react or behave similarly. Not all who suffer from the disease of alcoholism manifest the same symptoms. But there is one symptom of dependency that is almost universal: *denial*.

Alcoholism is probably the only disease that victims refuse to acknowledge they have and stubbornly resist recovery from. Even an alcoholic, when told by a physician that he or she has diabetes, will probably respond in the following way: "Thanks for alerting me. Please tell me what I can do to take care of myself, to avoid complications, and to alleviate the symptoms." Yet, informed by a doctor or loved one that he or she is addicted to alcohol, that same alcoholic is likely to respond in this way: "No way! Not me! You're wrong. What's the idea of trying to tell me how to live my life, anyway?"

The real tragedy of this is that almost all of us had strong suspicions that we were in trouble with alcohol. But we felt it was our business and that we could solve our own problems. We were determined not to share our secrets with outsiders.

The medical profession—both physicians and psychiatrists—often draw criticism for not being more knowledgeable about alcoholism. But it is characteristic of the alcoholic to reject any suggestion that he or she drinks too much, even when opinions come from experts on this disease. Active alcoholics are liable to lie to *anyone*, face-to-face. In recovery, many of us finally confess that we played clever tricks to cover the signs of our problem from medical professionals. For example, many of us would abstain from alcohol for a couple of days before a physical examination.

We followed doctor's orders regarding everything other than alcoholism; *we reserved our right to drink*. "Eternal evaders," we became masters of deceit. We guzzled in solitude and cleverly hid our bottles.

Behaving in an unrealistic manner is an alcoholic trait. Alcoholics invariably are overly sensitive, tense, and lonely. These character traits are common in dependency. Abhoring these perceived signs of "weakness," alcoholics tend to overcompensate by acting as independent and strong and gregarious as possible. This play-acting sets the stage for perpetual denial.

Even when we knew for a fact that we reeked of our alcoholic indulgences, we firmly denied the extent of our intake: "I had only a couple of small ones," we'd insist. This was usually enough to close the subject to further discussion with another person. Stubborn rejection of further discussions seemed justified to us because as we'd say time after time: "I'm me and it's my life; no one is going to tell me what I can or cannot do."

When alcohol sedated our brains, it also fed us erroneous messages that we were smart and clever. Numbed reflexes and impaired judgment assured us that we were right, self-sufficient, and sitting on top of the world. Everyone else was wrong.

Repeated denials are unmistakable symptoms of the grip alcohol has on the drinker. A drink is the most important thing in his or her life. But excess usually leads to a crisis; eventually we got into deep trouble. Our helpful friend, alcohol, deserted us when we most needed comfort. Then, in a return to helpless "childhood," we were reduced to complete dependency on *anyone* who would rescue us.

Unfortunately, we were not alone in practicing denial. Some of the people around us made it easy for us to escape grief. By bailing us out of painful situations and "fixing our mistakes," family members, friends, employers, and even some helping professionals denied us the opportunity to cultivate a new kind of thinking.

Sometimes, "helping hands" led us to conclude that, no matter how far we went in our troublemaking, someone would eventually come forward to save us the indignity and shame of "paying the piper." Fellow deniers who protected us reinforced our denial that there was any good reason to stop drinking.

There are good and natural reasons for a loved one to rush to the rescue of an alcoholic. "Why make him/her suffer more? He's/She's hurt enough." Alas, the spouses who stuck with us, the fellow workers who covered up for us, the lawyers who got us off easy—all probably believed in their hearts that they were clearing a path for us to change our behavior.

Sadly, even *threats* ultimately added to the benefits of denial. When the people in our lives forgave us one more time (again and again,) they were proving that they, too, were in denial. Their behavior had the effect of encouraging us to continue on with our uncontrolled drinking patterns.

Since everything was done for us, and not to us, our dependency on others increased. We deeply resented this. We came to deny that alcohol was our enemy. More and more, we directed our resentment and hatred at the very people who tried to help us. In our foggy minds, these people became the reasons for our problems with alcohol. Denial came full circle.

People-Pleasing

The typical heavy drinker on the way to alcoholism is likely to be a dedicated people-pleaser.

One recovering alcoholic said a great deal about people-pleasing very succinctly: *"I always was busy spending money I didn't have to buy things I didn't need to impress people I didn't like."*

For many of us, the need for approval and the desire for attention were driving forces behind our drinking behavior. To be noticed usually dominated our need for approval, since we could flaunt both our good and bad qualities in order to be seen and heard. Most of us made a display of either pride or guilt. Each, we thought, would be impressive to others. "Hey, man, look at little old me drinking everyone under the table." Or, "See what a hard-luck loser I am? Pity me."

We went to extremes, never realizing that the ideal behavior lies in the middle. That's the location of humility; we are neither too good nor too bad. That's why oldtimers in AA caution that "We are not saints" and, "There's no such thing as an utterly helpless drunk." With mock seriousness, some oldtimers give this advice to newcomers: "Just don't get too good by Thursday."

When we get sober, we eventually recognize pride-blindness in ourselves. We learn to guard against fantasizing a perfection we don't have and never will possess. Absolute perfection, of course, is not attainable. In arresting our alcoholism, we live more comfortably when we seek to be the best we can be and *improve*, rather than attempt to reach even the fringes of perfection. We have come to the conclusion that there is nothing wrong with visualizing a state of perfection, so long as it is simply an ideal toward which we can progress in coping with life.

Too many drinkers have stumbled through the progression of alcoholism *obsessed* with the idea that they can be the best drinkers in history. And being best means to them drinking all they want without losing control. "I can take it or leave it"; "I can lick any problem, even a drinking one"; "I'll quit when I decide it's time to quit."

Even when they have become addicted to alcohol, most people will persist in diligently practicing theories about control. But, sadly, drinking is probably the only endeavor in which the more one practices, the worse the performance becomes.

We people-pleasers ultimately became losers against our wishes. At booze fests, we imagined ourselves to be the life of the party, yet in reality we were *alone* with our own drinking patterns. When we breezed into bars, we were looking for opportunities to revel in our own generosity or the generosity of others. We'd invariably get involved in downing rounds of drinks. In these situations, both the "hosts" and the "guests" believed they were pleasing the people around us. "They let me buy them drinks because they like me," crows one. The other: "He wouldn't set 'em up for me if I didn't impress him."

Many barflies have gone to their graves or prison cells without recognizing the fact that they never made real friends while seated on a bar stool.

A prize example of this kind of delusion was chronicled in the news recently. An affluent New York City tippler, dead from liver disease, left $12,000 in his will to be divided between several of his favorite watering holes to buy drinks for the pals he'd left behind. At the time, his wife was quoted as saying: "Joe loved people and wanted them to love him. It's too bad he never found that love because he always was too drunk."

In contrast, love *is* found by recovering alcoholics in the group consciousness that comes when we gather to talk about the disease we have in common and ways of combating its compulsions and obsessions. We define love as the act of wishing good things for others.

For us, the best thing to wish others is serenity through sobriety. This concept makes it possible to love even those people we wouldn't necessarily choose as friends. Under this acceptance, we can find it quite natural to pray for those we resent.

Among the dangers of being people-pleasers is the risk of being rejected by the very people we strive to impress. The feeling of rejection is, itself, a strong enough emotion to send us scurrying for alcohol and the opportunity to obtain relief by drinking ourselves into oblivion. But rejection quickly leads to feelings of inadequacy, which in turn lead to self-pity or anger. And all these feelings are enemies of sobriety and serenity.

The best advice for would-be people-pleasers is to turn efforts toward helping people rather than impressing them.

■ ■ ■

Rationalizing

We alcoholics are experts at rationalization. We continually find it necessary to explain to others—and to ourselves—why we must continue drinking when every sign points to the fact that alcoholism is destroying us.

A rationalization is more than an excuse. It is an addict's serious effort to ascribe insane behavior to causes that seem entirely reasonable and valid but are, in truth, completely unrelated to reality. To rationalize is to scrounge frantically for a solid basis to a constant and stubborn denial of a problem with liquor.

We could be incredibly inventive with cover-ups when we were convinced that we must make the world understand why we failed time after time even when we were "on the wagon."

"I've got to drink to hold my job," we'd explain to some. "I can't refuse to drink with a client if I want to keep his business." "Drinking is as much an occupational hazard for me as wrecked knees are for football players." It was no consolation to us that not every heavy drinker is devoured by compulsive dependency. No alcoholic likes to believe that he or she is "weaker" than other people.

We rationalizers could not accept the fact that, should we carefully and seriously explain to friends or co-workers our physical inability to control our drinking, they would care little and would go on enjoying their grog without us.

"Impossible! They want me to share fun with them," we'd say.

When we looked forward with dry-throated anticipation to office parties, we found it natural to argue with our spouses that, "I have to make them like me at work or I'll stop getting those raises that keep you and the kids in plush comfort."

When we downed "a few" after work, rationalization assured us that the slugs were necessary to wipe away all the cares of the working day. After all, with those pressures and responsibilities, we merited sympathy, rather than criticism. What crosses we had to bear!

We would sing the same old refrain just as quickly if our jobs didn't have the challenges that would make our eight-hour day exciting. "You'd need to get sparked up, too, if you drudged in that boredom," we'd say.

Helpers in the field of alcoholism recovery have heard every variety of rationalization that exists. Few days go by without a counselor reminding a self-pitying alcoholic that no spouse ever turned a social drinker into a real drunk. And others cannot get him or her sober; only an honest desire to quit will work.

Rationalization usually forces "deniers" into manufacturing evidence that what they seem to be doing isn't as bad as it looks: "You've got me all wrong."

Even simple surgery can be a godsend to a drinker who can blame any physical behavior thereafter on a "doctor's bungling."

Defensive rationalization is intended to make a cover-up look realistic. Ruses can be clever. For instance, what could be wrong with a nonchalant indulger leaning against a wall or door frame at a party? Who could ever suspect this person is avoiding a swaying stance in the center of the room?

Then again, nobody should guess this same party-goer is being other than a helpful guest when he or she jumps at a chance to mix drinks for others. Of course, going alone into the kitchen to do so is above suspicion. The safest cover-up, naturally, is fortification at home *before* a party. Then, the crafty drinker can proudly show others how moderately he or she partakes.

Lighting a cigarette with a shaky hand? Who could doubt that the smoker has detected a draft when he or she uses both hands, cupped around the cigarette like a seasoned outdoorsman?

Sometimes we drinkers simply have to assert ourselves. A recovering alcoholic named George tells how his wife confronted him with a "test" she found in a book. Scoring of the test results apparently indicated that a person who could drink three drinks—no more, no less—at a specific time each day was a controlled drinker, not an alcoholic. George followed this routine for one week, then returned to an almost constant state of inebriation. When his wife countered his denials that he was alcoholic by reminding him that he'd ultimately failed the test, he replied with great indignation, "Baloney! I can pass that little old test...anytime I want to." Perfect rationalization!

■ ■ ■

Self-Pity

"Perfectionistic" and "hypersensitive" are words often used to describe an alcoholic. Perfectionism and hypersensitivity represent a danger-fraught emotional combination that kept us reaching for alcohol even when we knew it was killing us.

When the achievements that our perfectionistic minds had fantasized failed to materialize, our feelings were hurt. When we believed we had been rejected by life, fate, and friends, we felt the nagging need to be comforted. Experience had taught us that the most satisfying, readily available and fast-acting supply of comfort was contained in a bottle.

Self-pity can lead us to the grave, a mental institution, or prison if we continue to drown our sorrows. It also may drive us to take a drink—or take our own lives.

The companions of self-pity are feelings of rejection and inadequacy. They inspire more bitter tears and obsession to drink than any other unrealistic problem. Troubles that are pure fantasy die hard. Real troubles are seldom prolonged; the sufferer learns to either live with them or ignore them.

Imaginary problems erect blocks to effective action. The more we feel sorry for ourselves, the more we expect the world to change in our favor. We never see that it is we who must change. Fretting about rejections by people, places, and things builds a compulsion to seek sedation (escape from reality) through alcohol and pills.

Only when we got sober did it dawn on us that hours spent in regretting the unchangeable past and anticipating a future that may never happen simply sap the energy that could better be used in coping with the only time factor that counts—today.

The road to self-pity and rejection has been ably laid out by egotism and pride. Egotism, which is a luxury that we alcoholics cannot afford if we wish to live happily, is merely a craving for prestige, recognition, moral and monetary support, pampering, and special privileges. Liquor warped our judgment so extensively that we expected not only our "just dues," but more good things than others have.

Egotism also creates dependency on anticipated rewards. When these are not forthcoming, the rejection emotion sparks great anger. Hurt pride brings tears, all shed wholly for the "rejected" party. And we know that uncontrolled anger will almost guarantee another drunken binge.

A desire for perfection made us covet acclaim, success, social standing, and security. We insisted on being above criticism. Rampant egos made many of us sadistic, unsocial tyrants who were unwilling to share. Inwardly, we probably were afraid we were not capable of competing. We compared ourselves to others, expecting more than they. We became fault-finders, looking for imperfections in those whom we considered rivals. When they excelled, we were sure it was because luck was against us.

Feeling rejected by life, we submerged in self-pity. Our Big Me—Little You attitude changed to PLOM (poor little old me). Our hypersensitivity made each rejection hurt more and more. Every time we felt denied or deprived, it required more and more anticipated rewards to satisfy the greed of our egos. An ego never is satisfied. It becomes a tyrant, knowing no limits. Addiction to an ego is as possible as dependency on alcohol.

Self-pity seldom lasts forever, even with alcoholics. Too often, the emergence from this state of mind brings feelings of *guilt* and *shame*. We were also ashamed of being ashamed. We feared that our emotional binges would be discovered and we thus would be humiliated by having others lower their opinions about us.

To restrain the onslaught of the ego and pride that dominates, degrades, and dulls minds and breeds envy (stepping stone to rejection and self-pity), we need to recapture reality.

Coping with rejection and self-pity requires facing facts. Nobody, no places or things "out there," owes us support, duty, honor, or even respect. We have no right to make demands. Rewards are to be earned.

We know now that nothing and nobody outside ourselves got us drunk. Getting drunk was our very own achievement. It follows, then, that no one can rescue us, even if they yearn to do so. An extended hand is really all others can offer.The rest is truly up to us. We can rid ourselves of the worst moments of self-pity when we realize that our only rejection came from within us, not from outside.

Resentments

Here's one of the first things sobriety-seeking alcoholics are told: that the cultivation and harboring of resentments is the greatest single deterrent to the goal of total abstinence. Resentments of people, places, and things are normal reactions for the healthy as well as the sick. The dangers they present lie wholly in how much each resenter permits them to dominate him or her. Recovering alcoholics usually say that one of the *worst* parts of recovery is the constant rehearsal of resentments that they have for spouses, bosses, police, judges, doctors, psychiatrists, all "do-gooders," every form of detoxification and recovery center, and Alcoholics Anonymous.

So abundant is the crop of emotional pain from this particular character defect that advice about it constitutes almost a whole book of philosophy.

Resentment is double-edged, hurting the resenter much more than the resented. Any person who is the target of a resentment "owns" the one who hates him or her; unknowingly the target absorbs the best living time from a sick person whose primary concern should be recovering physically and emotionally.

It is often pointed out in the program that when the last two letters of the word *resentment* are removed, what remains is "resent me." This makes plain that the basis of resentment is our dislike of ourselves. Hence, a grumbling alcoholic may be told: "Maybe you'd better find out what is wrong with you that is making others seem obnoxious to you."

When we resent we actually are beating ourselves with clubs we thought we had reserved as weapons to attack others.

Primary objects of our resentment are people who don't live up to the pattern of behavior we expect of them. Alcoholics want to control everything around them. When we are denied that power, we leap into criticism. This naturally leads to an appetite for doting on rumors, gossip, fault-finding, jealousy, and rebellion.

It is a short step to intolerance. The "to hell with everyone else but me" kind of rebellion is basically self-pity in disguise.

When we are full of resentment we are turning our backs on humility and honesty, two essentials in recovery. Dishonesty breeds fear, an emotion that is the champion destroyer of peace of mind.

Within the world of resentment flourish jealousy, hatred, anger, and the urge for revenge. Distrust and fear drive the jealous person. The fear of losing—a threat to security and personal importance—builds anger and turns it toward others. This anger is the kind that seeks to hurt or destroy. The resultant loss of self-control overrides all reason.

In recovery we learn to consider any resentment a tragic waste of precious time, because it almost never gets beyond the mind of the hater and thus accomplishes nothing. Yet resentful alcoholics waste countless hours, days, and weeks that should be cherished as time available for practicing a recovery program. A life filled with resentment is a life of futility and unhappiness.

Resentment often is likened to a closed fist—a symbol of hostility. Troubled drinkers in the program are reminded that the friendly act of shaking hands is impossible when fists are clenched.

When we are faced with coping with a physical allergy coupled with an obsessive compulsion to drink, as all alcoholics are, we already have a monumental situation that needs all our concentration. It is therefore to be wondered how sane people can afford to handicap themselves in such a struggle by fouling up emotional control by being resentful.

In AA we are advised to solve a bellyful of resentments one at a time. We are told to list all such emotions fully, then honestly study each one in turn, erasing them singly before moving on to the next.

One now-sober alcoholic relates how he worked out a simple "allotment" system for resentments:

"I found myself quick to resent," he says. "I could easily fill a day with a bundle of them. So I decided to allow myself only one resentment per day."

This recovering man now begins each day with a reserve of one resentment. If the paper is late or he breaks a shoestring or the children have used all the hot water for showers, he consciously works at cutting short the temptation to flare into resentment.

"I don't want to waste my one big resentment for the day on something simple or nonsensical," he says with a smile. So as this man continues through his day, he encounters selfish motorists on the freeways, angry people on the telephone, and lousy service at lunch. But he always manages to save his resentment, he never wastes it.

"It is surprising," he says, "how often I go to sleep at night without having used up my resentment for the day."

■ ■ ■

Anger

For the person without a drinking problem, anger may be an emotional luxury. For the alcoholic, anger is emotional poison. People who are addicted to alcohol almost always have difficulty separating justifiable anger from anger that is unjustifiable.
    In recovery we force ourselves to surrender old ideas and thus accept the truth that anger is one of the four basic emotions common to all mankind. The other three are sadness, happiness, and anxiety. Anger is the least understood of all human sensitivities. And it is one that we don't often deal with appropriately.
    Anxiety and sadness are normal. They can even be directed toward usefulness rather than devastation. Society, however, has one quick answer to anger: you must never, never get mad. They might as well tell us to learn to live without breathing.
    Since we alcoholics always magnify any evidence of rejection, we are likely to lose the ability to accept everyday quirks of human nature. We quickly deduce that everybody "out there" considers us unworthy and objects of pity.
    In recovery, we find that all people must learn to cope with life. We were used to feeling we had no other way to curb anger than by drinking toward a comatose state.
    Anger plays no favorites. It can be incited by word or action, by a loved one as easily as by an enemy. Surely, outrage at God is the simplest act of anger.

Pretending not to get angry is a con job. If nothing else riles anger, there are Hamlet's "slings and arrows of outrageous fortune." Anger is normal; violent reaction to anger can be abnormal. Alcoholics do most things to excess. A *little* anger is a rarity for us.

Anger often is a useful component in living. Any schoolchild knows anger can spur self-protection. It fortifies people to resist being misused by others. Angry people overcome great odds and reach high goals when the emotion is controlled. Since anger tenses muscles and creates a gush of adrenalin, athletes can direct it toward victories or new world records.

Because anger helps one "fight back" it can be a weapon against enslavement. Dependency on any drug is a form of slavery. If angry enough, a drinker addicted to alcohol can escape that bondage.

Coping with anger covers many areas. A sense of humor can cut short anger and pave the way to "forget and forgive." A mere restraint of the tongue can create miracles of compromise and reconciliation. But anger not identified as such can build anxiety. Righteous indignation can destroy a person emotionally. One burst of temper can spoil a whole day. And anger that isn't dealt with can spoil sobriety.

Every recovering alcoholic has to grow emotionally. Resentments halt progress, and resentments are born from anger. Denying anger, refusing to "let it all hang out," brings on unreleased tension which overstimulates the nervous system. This condition paves the way for headaches, back pains, colitis, high blood pressure, ulcers, and even asthma attacks.

When we let anger possess us, the aftermath usually is deep guilt. This remorse leads to loss of self-regard, dejection, frustration, and fear. The next step backward is a feeling of worthlessness and helplessness. They are sobriety's worst foes.

Dealing with anger is not a one-step process. First, anger must be recognized as a normal reaction to be accepted with honesty and openness and not denial. "Sure, I got mad," the wise person admits.

Admitting our right to anger even if unjustified and without basis, we must get to the bottom of the flare-up. We find out what angered us.

Confining that anger to its source is vital. Otherwise it can spread to everybody and to all things. Unresolved anger is like a time bomb. It can blast in all directions. But it also can be defused.

Finally, anger must be worked off. In the past, we used to "drink it off." Recovering people cannot drink "at" anything. At least, anger must be nondestructive. Some flail a punching bag, some beat up on a pillow. The outlet to anger can be constructive. Much wood has been cut and many rooms painted by angry men and women.

As we grow in recovery, we begin to realize that many things that would have angered us in the past don't make us angry anymore. When we develop a conscious effort to consider the source of our anger, we often come to the conclusion that anger is not worth our time and energy. The most worthless use of anger is in reaction to the unreasonable and irrational behaviors of emotionally sick people.

Fear

One recovering alcoholic is fond of saying that no one else ever suffered as many torturous pains, calamitous disappointments, and devastating disasters as he had. Then, smiling, he explains further: "Only, none of those tragic experiences ever materialized. They were just the constant, fretful fears of things to come that my warped mind created while I was drunk."

It is difficult for nonalcoholics to understand how we abuse the normal emotion of fear. For us, fear will lead to despair and defeat, through horrendous binges, and into straight jackets, convulsive death, and even suicide. Alcohol has a way of magnifying every proverbial molehill into a towering mountain.

Without the fear response, humankind never could have survived. If we were fearless we would walk into trucks, touch high-voltage wires, and face wild animals with our bare hands. A well mind can control fear if there is no real danger. But, when alcohol has sickened the nervous system, often there is no choice about the control of either the fear or the intake of the liquid sedation which the drinker has learned will calm the troubled mind.

A recovering alcoholic knows alcohol is not to be feared. The fear is drinking it. Yet to millions of us, there came a grandiose ego that told us that the next drink need not be feared because we were sure we had control. It seldom occurs to us that freedom from fear is a perfection no one ever achieves—or needs.

Fear can be wisely used as a springboard to better living. It can inspire a respect for other people and for rules, and it can build an understanding of justice. Not even hate and resentment have to be destructive; such feelings can be accepted as experiences from which one may grow emotionally and morally.

Before recovery, we were inclined to make use only of the negative aspects of fear. We savored worry, uncertainty, evil thinking, and a dread of being hurt by people, places, and things. We were apprehensive of failure. Anxiety, the fear of the unknown, enveloped us. We connived to hide our drinking because we were afraid of disapproval and pity. We secreted bottles, not merely to deceive others, but because we were deathly afraid of hangovers, insomnia, and pain in all our disturbed body organs. We were well aware that alcohol's sedation alleviates suffering. So we feared the likelihood of ever being unable to readily find a jug at a time of desperate need.

Such negative thinking prevailed during most of our inbibing careers, but there can be a complete reversal to positive views after sobriety is achieved. Then, we learn the importance of caution, discretion, and self-preservation in confronting liquor.

When sober, we stop equating fear with cowardice. We also discover that seeking to remove all temptations is a waste of time and effort. The realization that temptation will always exist in life alerts us to the fact that we must not fear the temptation to drink. We accept the reality that a desire for alcohol may suddenly come anywhere and anytime. Our infallible defense is to fortify ourselves with the faith that we will be able to resist the drinking urge when it comes.

Fear has been defined as nothing more than a distorted faith in the negative. Fear goads us to expect only unpleasant, undesirable experiences. Hence, faith in the positive is an antidote to fear. When sober, we are able to have reliance, hope, and trust in our ability to resist the obsession to resume our drinking patterns. This attitude is nurtured and reinforced best when we regularly talk with others who have learned how to keep "the plug in the jug."

In sobriety we find that our fear and tension diminish when we remember that alcohol is not simply a beverage but a toxic poison for the man or woman who has become addicted to it. For us, no kind of liquor can be termed a "friendly enemy." Since there is no choice, there is less need to fear.

But to a great many abstaining alcoholics there is a constant fear of slipping—taking one drink that will ignite a chain reaction for more alcohol. This anxiety often is abated when we devote time to read and hear about just what alcohol is capable of doing to the body and emotions of those who have cultivated a dependency. Knowledge is a powerful weapon against an avalanche of fears.

Almost every recovering alcoholic has shattering, realistic dreams about drinking. The relief that comes when we awaken and realize that the nightmares were only nightmares is enough to make us thank our subconscious for doing us a great favor.

■ ■ ■
Hostility

Hostility is one of the most pronounced character defects in the alcoholic. Our raging anger and belligerence are reactions to our feelings of rejection and inadequacy.

When we were drinking, our hostility was both common and natural. We sensed uncloaked dislike from others throughout all the hours of our painful existence. Nonalcoholics didn't understand that we were not bad people who might become good; rather we were sick people who have a chance to get well. As we sensed other people's dislike of us and our behavior, we became ever more defensive. Doctors who are familiar with alcoholism recognize and contend with the public attitude that holds the drunk entirely responsible for his condition and deserving of no sympathy. In an issue of the *Journal of the American Medical Association*, Marvin A. Bloch, M.D., pointed out that, while a "psychiatric patient may be regarded by society with fearful distrust, an alcoholic is confronted with open hostility and condemnation."

Dr. Bloch found that this attitude always is so clear to patients undergoing rehabilitation that they treat rejection as a matter of course. Thus they build a giant barricade to acceptance of help from others.

We have all learned through experience that the one sure thing that can bring us escape from such social ostracization is more alcohol. All too often, we were pushed into another drunk as a way to tolerate everyone who was "against" us.

Even those persons closest to us came to expect us to behave so abnormally that the symptoms of a relapse may not have been obvious until we had retrogressed to the point of disaster.

Even our total abstinence can be beyond the belief of others. They have seen us "potted" so consistently that they not only are surprised at this avoidance of the bottle, but look on with suspicion. "What's the lush trying to pull on us this time?"

The label "alcoholic" usually is repugnant to any heavy imbiber. We wanted to escape that designation. Others readily accept us as "normal" in all modes of behavior other than intake of alcohol. So it was not surprising that we assumed that there really was nothing abnormal about our drinking—*when we remembered to be cautious*. Our befuddled minds told us it was a simple matter to prove we weren't weirdo barflies.

We reasoned: "If I can just control the amount consumed, it will be easy to show everybody that I'm a social drinker who sometimes likes to have fun." So we tried to impress others. And our world caved in.

Most alcoholics start out with a keen desire to find "something new and different" from hum-drum existence. We were forever striving "to belong" with folks who were not in a rut. We nurtured an urge to pursue pleasure. Above all, we sought quick and sure relief from distress. We sought sedation. And alcohol is a drug that is a sedative, an anesthetic, a soporific, and a depressant.

It is natural for anyone to want a life that is relatively free of stress. But for us alcoholics, the simple wish to "feel good" was our ticket to alcoholism. The "good feeling" (a freedom from stress and worry) was a "gift" we received from alcohol. But the gift didn't last. And following epi-

sodes of "feel good" drinking, the problems we were trying to escape returned, oftentimes more complicated than they'd been before. Nobody understood us and somehow we never achieved that carefree "good life" we sought. We felt that we had been cheated and let down. We felt let down because our wish to be different originated from a seething puddle of anxiety, pain, depression, frustration, boredom, and loneliness. We became hostile. And we became addicted.

■ ■ ■

The Gift of Humility

Admitting that we are powerless over alcohol and can no longer manage our lives is the first, and most difficult, decision we must make before we can hope to attain and hold on to sobriety.

This is referred to as the act of surrender. Before surrender is possible, however, we must find humility. The need for humility continues all the days in the lives of those who must control an incurable addiction through total abstinence.

After getting sober, we do a great many things we never did while drinking. We bring home our paychecks, show up at weddings and anniversary parties and stay sober at them, walk past bars, and stay out of jail, among other things. But such admirable behavior does not warrant our pinning medals on our own chests. In true humility, we tell ourselves that millions of men and women without this disease have been doing these expected things for years.

Since we specialize in self-wills run riot, humility is not come by easily. Too often, alcoholics consider the word *humility* to be synonymous with weakness of character. How far from "humble pie" true humility is. Basically, it is the state of being teachable. Actually, if humility did stem from humiliation, we would have no trouble grasping it; for years, we have been humiliating ourselves through embarrassing and obnoxious behavior.

Humility may be explained as the absence of aggressive self-assertion. Its first cousin is honesty. Together, these qualities bring about an open mind—the willingness to learn truths.

Through humility, we find the ability to evaluate conditions as they really are, especially in identifying our primary problem as alcoholism. Confronting this kind of reality and electing to cope with it kicks the props out from under arrogant pride. As we get sober, we effect down-to-earth relationships with others.

Humility is an antidote for pride-blindness, that state of mind that encourages us to imagine for ourselves a lot of perfections we don't possess. This distortion of pride permits us to feel superior to others who, too, are having problems. The surprising thing about pride-blindness is the ease with which it is developed and justified. Through it, anything will seem right in the eyes of the "down-the-hatch" guys and gals.

Humans can never attain absolute humility. Perfection in anything can only be ingrained. But progress in humility is possible and desirable. Those of us who know what "progress" means will settle gladly for humility for just today. We grow emotionally because we recognize ambition as a sincere desire to live usefully through a sense of humility.

Healthy humility makes it easy to say, "I'm sorry." Apologizing is not humiliating. It is a sign of maturity. If the apology isn't prompted by sincere contrition it won't benefit the person who wishes to make amends and will bring discomfort to both giver and receiver. Humility, however, lets apologies be done with dignity. "Do it standing straight, not down on your knees."

Yet, we know that making amends is a "must" act if we are to know happy, comfortable sobriety. Clearing away wreckage of the past is a part of the spiritual and emotional growth that fortifies serenity in sobriety. Merely being "dry" is not enough in the rugged world of coping with adversities. We still have problems; we just can't "solve" them by getting sloshed. Fighting compulsions, we call on humility to remind us we cannot do it alone and need advice from other sober drunks. Humility is also the best known safeguard against depression.

Because we alcoholics are masters of faulty rationalization, we must guard against misinterpreting the humility we have found in recovery. We are in trouble if we believe that we have our disease licked and that humility has somehow given us an edge over others or a "pipeline to God." Reminding ourselves that humility started the process of recovery keeps us from living with both feet firmly planted in midair.

■   ■   ■

Becoming Grateful

A grateful alcoholic rarely gets drunk.

This statement is as close to an absolute as the complex disease of alcoholism can support. This statement also serves to emphasize the fact that recovery through total abstinence takes more effort than emptying bottles down a drain and staying out of bars.

In order to maintain our often hard-won sobriety, we must, above all else, be thankful that we have learned the only way to head off impending doom: don't take the first drink.

Regardless of how much ingratitude we feel over a lack of material, emotional, or spiritual "gifts," and regardless of the bad luck we've had, our most potent protection of serenity and sobriety is to quote a familiar cliche: compared to what? In sobriety we reiterate, "The worst day of my life while sober is infinitely better than the very best day I ever thought I was enjoying when drunk."

This gratitude for an improved way of life makes it possible for us to readily accept the cold realities of our disease. Less and less frequently are we likely to wring out the crying towel of self-pity and moan, "Why me?" *Whys* do not matter to those who accept and feel gratitude that the agony has ended.

It is difficult for anyone to be unhappy while he or she is grateful. At the first signs of self-pity, we should be quick to count our gratitudes: not shaking while trying to shave or drink a cup of coffee, waking up instead of coming to each morning; not wallowing in a jail drunk tank; not looking frantically for the car after a blackout; not finding that our bags were standing packed on the lawn when we finally made it home...and countless more blessings.

The vast majority of us can be grateful simply for the fact that we are still alive, when by all the odds of fate and nature we would be in the morgue had we continued to drink.

The most useful form of gratitude, however, does not look backward and shudder over the might-have-beens. *Today's* living is the favorite target for our gratefulness. Then comes gratitude that tomorrow has a far greater chance of being good than had any past tomorrows when we were drunk. Thus is born the positive thinking that all lasting recoveries must have.

Gratitude is an antidote for superegotism. Recovering alcoholics cannot afford the handicap of "bigshotism." We must cope with the good as well as the bad, success along with failures. Self-control grows with an open-minded acceptance of disagreeable experiences. But we need to guard against being inflated into imbalance by material gains, achievements, and elevated importance.

We alcoholics tend to revel in personal triumphs. Any unexpected prosperity can motivate a desire to celebrate by drinking, as easily as rejection will spur the impulse to "drown our sorrows in suds."

Gratitude comes more readily when we think of ourselves as people whose misfortunes have brought good fortune. We are grateful that we have one big thing going for us: we can use our change in character from faulty to healthy to help other drinkers who are suffering the same despair from which we have escaped. When we are truly grateful, the successes we have in helping others are a fortunate bond of identification, not a power that calls for a feeling of self-satisfaction.

Nonalcoholics constantly are puzzled at how recovering alcoholics laugh in relating the embarrassing things they did while stoned. We laugh gratefully to fortify against any possible desire to return to past behavior.

Many seekers-for-sobriety consider gratitude the key to recovery since it reduces the birth of resentments. "It is hard to hate when you are grateful," they hear from oldsters. "Let us love you until you have learned to love yourself."

As alcoholics, we learn lessons the hardest ways possible. So by considering sobriety a "gift," we shield ourselves from our tendency for self-congratulations, a reaction that leads to complacency—and perhaps a return to the bottle.

Gratitude fortifies patience, a quality vital in recovery. Instant serenity is a rarity. So we are reminded that God might not give us more than we want, but He surely will let us have all the good things we can handle comfortably.

How to cultivate gratitude? It usually develops best when we discuss our problems with fellow alcoholics.

■　■　■

Our Insanities

One of the questions every recovering alcoholic is sure to ask himself or herself at one time or another is this: "How could I have behaved like that? I must have been crazy." Once we sober up, it seems incredible to us that we had totally lost control of our alcohol intake.

This state of temporary insanity is old hat to recovering alcoholics and experts who study the brain processes of problem drinkers. Alcohol long has proved its ability to so scramble the normal processes of an intoxicated person's brain.

Men and women under the influence of alcohol have said goodbye to the natural instinct of self-preservation. An alcoholic is determined to drink at any cost. This violates the basic principle of sanity—the will to survive.

Any drinker who persists in challenging the omnipotence of his enemy, alcohol, is as stubbornly gullible as the worker who loses a finger testing for himself the danger he has been told lies in a whirring buzz saw. And the worker is no more sane than the disbelieving alcoholic if the finger-loser tries to explain what happened by saying, "I only stuck a finger up there and—wow, there goes another one."

For so long, we refused to profit by experience. Why should we? We were desperately ill; sick bodies seldom house healthy minds.

When nonalcoholics recover from a binge, they readily admit to their drunken insane behavior. Their minds, not warped by persistent drinking, can face reality and analyze in a normal manner.

It is natural for problem drinkers who may truthfully protest, "I'm as normal as anyone when I'm not drunk," to resent references to alcoholic insanity. They are quick to overlook the crazy things they did *while* intoxicated.

We who vehemently deny should ask ourselves what it is, if not insanity, that forced us to take that "first drink" when every fiber of our bodies was repulsed at the prospect of the physical pain and mental anguish it would start. Every sober alcoholic knows he or she is only one drink away from a drunk.

When we were drinking, we always came up with reservations about every sane, honest effort to quit. Dodging the truth always further distorted our already sick thinking. Sane reasoning is possible only when we recognize and accept the fact that the mind of every alcoholic is made unstable by alcohol.

When we admit to our insanity, the only thing that is hurt is our false pride. We must admit fully. Partial acceptance is useless. We must prevent our pride from continuing to equivocate: "In one kind of way, I'm alcoholic"; "Maybe I am a little bit"; "I might be a borderline case"; "Well, I guess it's possible."

Without free exercise of self-criticism, reality is denied. Hence there is no honest evaluation of our problem. On the other hand, awareness of alcohol's power to nurture insane behavior brings hope, willingness, and faith.

The spiritual phase of Alcoholics Anonymous's program puts early stress in the Twelve Steps on the alcoholic being restored to sanity. This happens only when one stops drinking.

In the program we are reminded that it is a misconception that alcoholism is only a symptom of a deeper-seated emotional disorder. Some of us have wasted many years in trying to cure something mysterious that is hidden (and may never be found) instead of confronting the surface truth that alcoholism is a disease—a physical dependency and addiction coupled with a compulsion.

Anyone can become an alcoholic. People with vastly different backgrounds, experiences, and lifestyles become alcoholics. But regardless of the very real differences that exist among them, people who are alcoholic manifest similar symptoms and drinking behavior patterns. Although some mentally disturbed people do become alcoholics, it could be said that alcohol causes insane behavior; insanity doesn't cause alcoholism.

■   ■   ■

Stinkin' Thinkin'

While rationalizing the need to continue drinking, we alcoholics indulge in a unique brand of reasoning that is referred to as alcoholic thinking. In the book, *Alcoholics Anonymous*, we read that alcohol can be personified with traits such as "cunning, baffling, and powerful." Some members add "jealous and patient." What this means, of course, is that the strong subconscious compulsion to ingest alcohol nudges at the awareness of the alcoholic. The compulsion nudges the alcoholic until he or she is absolutely *convinced* that an alcoholic drink is a life line, a vital necessity for happy comfort.

So comes a flight to the clouds, propelled by swigs from the bottle. Always, there follows the nosedive to a devastating crash-landing. Recounting the "bright ideas" that kept us drinking helps us remember what being restored to sanity means.

One problem drinker, for example, stubbornly contended that he was strictly a normal and unspectacular drinker. But always, when drinking at home, he would climb to the upper branches of a walnut tree in his front yard so that he had the freedom to drink as he chose without being observed or berated by wife and pals. After all, nobody ever looks up in a tree for a social drinker.

There are many more stories. One long-ago Tuesday, a "blackout artist" came awake in a motel in southern California. He had money and a thirst. But it was election day and a since-repealed law kept all bars and liquor stores closed on voting days.

But what sly, clever alcoholic ever failed to get his drink? Just think rationally! In Nevada, there was no crazy election-day law. There was nothing insane about a guy flying to Las Vegas, buying a couple of jugs, and returning to Los Angeles on the next plane. Which is what "our hero" did. With much pride.

A certain recovering alcoholic tells of how she used great logic when she was tippling. Embarrassed at having to sneak out after midnight and cram her empty bottles deep in the trash barrels of neighbors (people already had talked about her own rubbish being bottle-heavy) she talked her husband into moving. They went to live in a cantilever house whose back windows overlooked a deep canyon. What a graveyard for "dead rum soldiers."

Another woman could never see anything unusual in the fact that, deep in her cups, she tried to shoot herself in the head one desperate night—and was so unsteady that she missed her temple and sent a bullet into her husband's thigh. "Just a crazy, unlucky accident," is how she described it.

Nor could an alcohol-confused gent ever think it strange that he was accustomed to slamming shut his car door while his head still was inside. "That blasted door got sprung off balance when I hit a tree," he explained.

The fear of the unknown and the inflated anxieties that result are common to all stinkin' thinkin' drinkers. "I constantly was clearing away the wreckage of my future," is how one sober alcoholic explains the days of her romance with the bottle.

Explaining uncontrolled behavior became an art for us. As one man said, "I didn't want to drink that whole bottle but, my God, somehow the cap got lost and I didn't want the contents to evaporate.'' Now that's stinkin' thinkin'.

■   ■   ■

What Sobriety Takes Away

Faced with the reality that we have an incurable disease that can be arrested only with total abstinence from alcohol, our first reaction to the idea of giving up our "friendly drug" was dismay: "You mean I can never again know the joys of getting smashed?" "Do I really have to give up that liquid refresher with its cozy sensations—and all my fun-loving drinking buddies besides?"

Our sacred right to let liquor trickle down our gullets is not all we give up when sober. Like celebrators on New Year's Eve making resolutions, we can, at the start of a new life in sobriety, recount some of the surrendered horrors that we will be happy to see fade into the irretrievable past.

Gone, for example, is the frenzy of a frantic and breathless rush on the morning after an alcoholic blackout to see if the automobile is in the garage and has no newly created fender dents or, worse yet, blood on the bumper.

Gone is the inability to get the first several morning slugs to stay down until one finally "catches" and begins to placate the jitters. Absent, too, may be the impulse to throw up while brushing our teeth.

In sobriety we give up the trick of driving on winding roads with one eye closed so that the center line will look to be only the necessary one—instead of the two from double vision.

No longer will we need to sleep in a drunken stupor on the cool bathroom floor so the depository will be readily accessible when the stomach revolts time and again during the night.

Giving up alcohol also takes away the chilling experience of staggering home at daybreak to find our bags packed and planted firmly on the front lawn.

No more will there be the thrill of living bountifully through many "lit-up" weeks on credit cards and the electrifying shock at seeing the totals on the monthly statements.

Sobriety may stop that constant variety of jobs won and lost. We will have to tolerate uninterrupted weekly paychecks, be reconciled to regular salary increases, and be forced to discover that the boss is not an incarnation of Satan after all.

We relinquish the endless excitement at having checks bounce, charge accounts canceled, and fine automobiles repossessed.

Flatly rejected are the prospects of countless nights spent in flop houses, on grassy lawns and park benches, in gutters or alley crates, or even on hard floors of drunk tanks. The ex-drunk must be satisfied with clean sheets on mattresses, night after night.

Soberness forces us to give up solitude and loneliness. We'll have to suffer along with genuine love from friends and family.

In recovery we walk away from the delights of periodically drying out in alcoholic wards of hospitals and jails. Gone too are the massive injections and handfuls of prescribed pills.

We part ways with bar pals who used to pick us up when we fell off those bar stools or who mopped away blood and counted our lost teeth after brawls. Sobriety also reduces our contact with the straight lines we must prove we can walk and breatholaters into which to blow for the men in blue.

When excessive drinking is given up, so too are the clamps to prevent tongue-swallowing during convulsions. Farewell to playmates in delirium tremens that look like man-sized spiders or purple snakes. No more falling-down accidents or burning beds set afire during drunken smoking. Goodbye to the chills and shakes of withdrawal. Surrendered will be the skull-splitting headaches, cotton-coated tongues, dizzy nausea, and dry heaves that make up the joyful world of the hangover.

We also relinguish the need to ask forgiveness from our spouses and children whom we may have slapped around. No more reason to helplessly sob to our spouses, "I'll never take another drink."

The list of things sobriety takes away goes on and on, but replacements for things lost are obvious and oftentimes life-transforming. Perhaps the best new "thing" in the recovering person's life is the sense of gratitude that develops when he or she realizes the simple fact that not drinking can clear away much of the wreckage of the past.

Willingness

The active alcoholic who decides to "taper off" by gradually exerting more and more self-control can be compared to the novice who pits himself against a judo expert. Just as the trained combatant helps the unskilled foe defeat himself by pulling when the other pushes and pushing in response to pulls, alcohol builds fantasies while employing its addictive powers to devastate the body and emotions.

In recovery we readily admit that alcohol remained the undefeated champion of our world for all the years of our drinking. Even though generations before us found that liquid enemy cunning, powerful, and baffling, acceptance of reality must come for each of us as individuals before we can see the truth that we are badly overmatched.

Willingness is the starting point for the switch from a life of intoxication to one of sobriety. Willingness, in an all-out sense, is surrender to reality. And, without a willingness to keep the plug in the jug, there can be no peace of mind for the alcoholic.

Willingness is no more than a humble compliance to the rules of the sobriety game. As we've said before, this game, which one must play to win, has but a single rule, which is the same as the name of the game: Don't Drink.

We suffering drunks headed for sobriety must take the first step forward by admitting we are bankrupt in every area of living. We may be surprised to realize that this admission makes us humble. Humility, in turn, breeds a feeling of need. This desire will open the door for willingness.

These character changes constitute a lot for confused boozers to grasp quickly. But they can be had. Only one decision on our part can lose precious willingness, desire, need, and humility. The one careless idea that will destroy the whole kaboodle is: "Man, I've really done it. I'm cured." Then the horrifying toboggan slide may be only a few steps away.

The first gift of abstinence, of course, is sobriety. It will be the most important result of avoiding liquor, but it is not the only reward. If sobriety were all that recovering alcoholics received, we would be like the man who buys a seat at a $100-a-plate dinner and eats only the olives. Recovery is a banquet.

Abstinence opens the way to growth. In contrast, when a person stops growing emotionally, dying begins.

We don't need to make our disease a lifetime burden. It is simple and easy for us to live with the truth that the disease is incurable, but arrestable. But we must never forget that fact. To forget is to invite the cork to pop magically from the bottle of liquor.

Remembering our dependence on alcohol keeps us aware that we have one primary rule for living each day: don't take that drink. Where once we would have considered abstinence a morbid thought, we now happily tell ourselves that as long as we don't guzzle, we will have no fear of a dreadful hangover the next morning. We look forward to most days.

So as recovering alcoholics we know contentment, but we dread getting smug or complacent. Experience has shown us that it takes so little (a bottle of beer, a split of wine) for the overconfident person to buy a long ride on a spinning merry-go-round.

Many experts argue against trying to achieve complete peace of mind. Recovering alcoholics are like all emotionally growing people; they are never satisfied for long intervals. How can we grow and learn if we are satisfied?

We need not get sober to find peace of mind. We got that quickly by downing buckets of booze. Thus sedated, we forgot dissatisfactions and even being alive. But this false serenity was temporary.

During our recovery, we actually find total abstinence means not accepting anything as perfect. If we fight and lose, we learn. Learning also comes from winning fights. But nobody fights by lying on a feather bed. Action is the magic word.

Life at its fullest brings changes in a person. Sober alcoholics usually seek to learn and grow from handling the worries, concerns, problems, unrest, struggles, and dissatisfactions of living. The willingness we speak of is a willingness to be realistic while striving for continued sobriety and growth. This effort is the balancing act called life.

■ ■ ■

Our Obsession

Many sober alcoholics prefer to identify themselves as "recovering" rather than "recovered." In recovery, we come to understand that we are only one drink away from a drunk and that the obsession that kept us drinking can revive the desire for a drink at any time during our sobriety.

After we have arrested the drive of our dependency, the obsession ordinarily leaves, sometimes quickly, and frequently after months or even years of abstinence.

But some degree of a needling tendency may persist. This has been described as suppressed impulse, well-preserved temptation, hidden desire, chemical coercion, emotional pressure, deceptive urge, crafty incitement, even a mental seduction.

Whatever it is, the undercover "awareness of alcohol's potential" functions in a manner that is universally called cunning, baffling, powerful, jealous, and patient. In ways that often seem sinisterly mysterious, the urge known as "the thirst" continues to subtly remind the brain of the wonders wrought when the belly is full of hootch.

The dependency on alcohol acts on the mind of the problem drinker like a confidence man who really doesn't sell phony items to the sucker, but rather, instills such a greed that the victim literally begs to be let in on a larcenous deal.

Without constant vigilance our defenses are vulnerable. Our obsession may be compared to a crafty football quarterback who, sensing that a certain play won't work again, fakes that play and throws a different manuever at the opponents. Once we alcoholics, no matter how long we have been sober, are tricked into thinking we can and should resume drinking, our "defensive line" has been hoodwinked.

An alcoholic who is intent on maintaining total abstinence may become irritated, angry, confused, exhausted, and even desperate through resisting the urge if he or she fights the battle without help. In such a condition, all it may take is the simple, "reasonable" idea that one little drink will straighten out his or her thinking. After all, when the drinker once thought it possible to control intake, liquor was a comforting elixir that brought oblivious escape from travails.

The ego of the alcoholic is a prime target for the hidden compulsion. Its capacity for inflation is great. When we were drinking, progression toward the "first drink" was usually marked by our complete confidence that we remained the master of all our destinies. We were sure that nobody was smarter than we. We were convinced that every success in our lives was our doing alone. Every failure was bad luck or interference by those "guys out there."

Resistance and denial flourish in the alcoholic mind as the temptation grows. We rationalized: Me an alcoholic? How can I be when I'm not on skid row, in a drunk tank, or locked in an asylum? That's where drunks are found. Not between silk sheets. Why, I'm still holding my job. My spouse hasn't left me. I drink to live up to my popularity. I'd let all those pals down if I went on the wagon. Look at the fun I'd miss. Hell, everybody drinks. Oh, maybe I down a little more than the average, but I've got great capacity. Sobriety? That would bore me to death. What would I do with my leisure time? To please the hecklers, I'll cut down. Maybe tomorrow. Or next week. I can do it whenever I decide it's time.

If anyone suggested that we should find out the nature of our drinking, we were insulted. With surprised indignation, we reasoned craftily: Next, you'll tell me to go to Alcoholics Anonymous. Those religious freaks. Fanatics on the God stuff. Probably a branch of the WCTU. A bunch of reformers and do-gooders. As long as I know how to taper off when necessary I don't need that sort of thing.

Usually, a sarcasm trip came next under the goading of the obsession to drink. The lines are old and familiar: So you think I should quit drinking? What kind of a mouse do you think I am, anyway? I suppose I ought to go all the way in getting reformed. Quit smoking. Diet away my pot belly. Start jogging. You want me to stop joking? Do away with laughs and fun parties? Walk out on all my friends? Is that what you want me to become?

This type of thinking can be stored inside our minds even after we are sober and the obsession to drink has left us. Perhaps. No matter how many protective coverings we have created, the compulsion may crouch, ready to spring forth once a weakness causes the letdown of barriers. One wide open invitation to drinking again comes when we conclude, "I might as well be drunk if I'm going to feel this miserable."

Even when a major recovery hurdle is met and cleared, the strength and deviousness of a lurking desire may spark an even more cunning train of thought. It all goes something like this: "I've already got my booze problem solved. My sobriety is top level and solid. I'm cured. Why don't I relax? I've shown my frightened family and apprehensive friends that abstinence isn't all that difficult for me to handle." Simply stated, this is another example of stinkin' thinkin'.

■ ■ ■

The Dry Drunk

At one time or another, almost every recovering alcoholic suffers the discomfort of a "dry drunk." These emotional disturbances may occur many times over the years. The period of time these disturbances last may vary greatly.

The goal of most persons concerned with the arrest of the disease of alcoholism, whether it be we drunks or those who help us get rid of the compulsion and dependency, is a 180 degree change in character and behavior for the alcoholic.

So important does it usually become for us to make that complete turn into a "new man" or a "new woman" that we may be dismayed and frustrated following any self-evaluation that tells us our progress is moving in low gear.

Very soon after we have begun the total abstinence that is the only means of recovery, we realize how abnormal were our attitudes and actions when we were bombed out of our skulls. Hence, when we realize or are told by others that we are the same old bundle of character defects sober that we were when intoxicated, it is natural to take a trip into a "dry drunk" state of mind.

What sometimes depresses recovering alcoholics is that we cannot always detect any steady, measurable positive changes. We are living without the crutch of alcohol. We are discouraged because our shortcomings still persist.

We may be depressed or "edgy" although we've been without a drink for months or years. When this happens, it is usually found that we are trying to "cure" ourselves through our own efforts. Men and women who "go on the wagon" without advice or identification with others and who treat alcoholism as a bad habit that will power is enough to shoo away, are usually as hard to live with as before the plug went in the jug. In fact, we may be even more unpleasant. How familiar are the words: "I think I liked you a lot better when you were drinking."

The word *intoxication* is from the Greek word for "poison"; the alcoholic on a dry drunk is being poisoned by a state of mind, a mode of behavior, a lack of well-being.

In a dry drunk we demonstrate the worst traits of alcoholics. We may flaunt grandiose behavior. We exaggerate our own capabilities, judgment, and intelligence to an unrealistic point where we can be anything from ridiculous to cruel.

Our faulty judgment frequently makes us harsh on ourselves. We may feel totally unworthy. We make up for that by criticizing others so severely we become obnoxious. Impatience takes over and makes us dissatisfied with others and the whole world. When nothing comes quickly, we display indignation.

Most alcoholics are emotionally immature. So it is reasonable that a dry drunk can lead to childish behavior. The road is from boredom to petulance, from distraction to disorganization. Changes in mood happen from minute to minute. Enthusiasm is short-lived, hence the sufferer becomes dissatisfied with life itself.

Usually, when we're on a dry drunk, we do not know why we are uncomfortable. Preservation of self-esteem makes us say, "I could never be that kind of jerk," while

we secretly know our behavior is far from what we want it to be.
   Self-doubt brings a need to bolster our self-esteem. We see in everyone around us the same faults that trouble us. We point out, "Look, I'm no different from anyone else." This attitude leads to projection into "fears of the unknown." We rationalize that others want us to get drunk. We are sure they already suspect us of drinking. Our reasoning is that those bad-wishers in our world of sobriety want us to slip off the wagon because they secretly are drinking. This overreaction spills over into the small things of living, like being unable to start the car.
   Dry drunks do not necessarily lead to real binges. But it happens. Families and friends, who always suffer most, must strive to avoid discouragement, confusion, depression, resentment, and bitterness. Usually a family member is least effective in snapping us out of a dry drunk. We may even retaliate drastically. Help from outside is the ideal answer, especially if it comes from alcoholics who have gone through dry drunks.

Shaking the effects of a dry drunk can be a relatively simple process if the victims can be shown the way to humility. Only then will we be ready and able to admit that we are not blameless sad sacks who have been attacked by the world around us. Self-discipline usually accompanies ego deflation. When we're suffering from a dry drunk, we need involvement with other people who genuinely want the same kind of serenity that we desire. People who are ready to accept help are much more likely to get help.

Why Slips Happen

Many of us recovering alcoholics will at some time experiment with controlled drinking—with various degrees of disaster— before becoming convinced that we can never safely drink again. Total abstinence is our only hope when dealing with the incurable disease of alcoholism.

In recovery programs such as Alcoholics Anonymous, relapses are referred to as "slips." In that fellowship we contantly hear agonizing reports of slips which may last only a day or continue for weeks, months, and years before a return to sobriety. Sometimes death or insanity intercedes.

"Slippers" always are welcomed back for another try by AA and other groups without scoldings. Many of us with long sobriety have gone that route and know how the returnee feels. The usual advice is, "The door swings both ways." But the "slipper' is cautioned not to take for granted that the "in" door always will work for him or her.

Those who choose to "go out and lay more track" just to rediscover for themselves if it's true they cannot drink, are cautioned: "Of course you have another drunk in you, but you may not have another recovery."

To nonalcoholics, the slip may be frustratingly mysterious. They ask why any man or woman with newly found sobriety would sacrifice serenity, health, peace of mind, and self-respect for the effects one drinking session may afford.

Many in sobriety claim that there is no such thing as a "slip"— that the drinking spree has been slowly built up in the alcoholic's mind until suddenly, seemingly unexpectedly, it happens.

One thing is certain; we are only one drink away from a drunk. A single drink can immediately start a prolonged drunken bout. This does not always happen, but it usually is more dangerous if the "experimenter" gets by with the first try. Tentative success will raise doubts: "Maybe I'm not really an alcoholic"; "I guess I've got it made"; "Wow, I'm cured." The quantity of drinking may well increase unhampered. The long, long binge may be close at hand.

Researchers on alcoholism have reduced causes for slips to four general reasons: (1) rebellion, (2) a belief that the problem is gone, (3) carelessness, and (4) complacency. Of course, there can be purely physical reasons— illness, exhaustion, anxiety, and depression among them. A sick mind often tells the addict that alcohol is needed for medication.

Self-induced pressure about success with sobriety can also make us susceptible. Mulling over thoughts like "I've just got to make it; I can't afford to fail," puts us in a spot where any minor setback will send us in search of a bottle.

Feelings of guilt often prolong a slip. Thinking "I'm a no-good weakling; what's the use?" keeps us on a downward spiral. *Regret* about a setback does little harm, but guilt is likely to block the growth of the self-forgiveness that is necessary to spur another try for sobriety.

For alcoholics, the best teacher is adversity. When we accept a slip as only a temporary setback, we can use it to fortify the strength of character needed to again seek help to quit drinking.

It is natural for us to remember how expertly alcohol eased all pain. Such recall may impel us carelessly into a new search for sedation when pain mounts. It is easy to forget that alcohol is not a permanent painkiller. Its relief is short-lived. The subsequent return to pain is more intense than before.

Lack of humility and a magnified intolerance can make us susceptible to a slip. Yet these defects come to full bloom in us mainly because our addictiveness and compulsions have become greater than ordinary. Our emotional stress is harder to control.

We alcoholics tend to scoff at rules. We rebel easily, not because we are alcoholics but because we are human. Everyone is irked by restrictions. Nobody likes to be restrained, prohibited, negated. But escape for us lies in the bottle. That escape can kill us. Any "slipper" starts unrealistic rationalizing long before a relapse.

Most of our emotional difficulties are shared by all mankind and are not unique to us. But because we are addictable and compulsive, we must live constantly on the defensive. Our reactions to our perceived limitations will continue to frustrate us unless we do the following: work a complete program of recovery; attend to our relationship with a Higher Power; let go of resentments; and maintain our sobriety and serenity a day at a time.

■ ■ ■

Loneliness

One of the amusing quips that recovering alcoholics direct at drinkers who are unsure about whether or not they're alcoholic is this: "Keep coming back (to our rap sessions) until you can decide; you won't catch the disease from us because it's not contagious."

Because alcoholics also like to call their disease the disease of loneliness, those quipsters might well be told that this part of their disease must be infectious, since loneliness is a universally common ailment.

Any probe into the subject of loneliness may start with the alcoholic as the perfect example. From every direction, we are crowded toward loneliness. Friends ridicule, denounce, damn, coddle, and rant at us. We are tolerated, shunned, ignored, and misunderstood by the public. The law berates, pities, and tries to shame us to sobriety through punishment. Doctors and psychiatrists observe, question, hospitalize, inject, medicate, and advise us before giving up in frustration. The clergy prays for us and begs us to repent. Loved ones weep for us, plead with us, and threaten and protect us with equal fervor.

To some degree, all alcoholics dwell in loneliness, sharing a world with remorse, guilt, doubt, rejection, low self-esteem, defeat, fear, discouragement, worry, inadequacy, and self-pity, to name only a few of our "friends." In the past we knew only one savior, the bottle. It alone could dissolve all pain and misery.

No person ever deserts a drunk as completely as we drunks deserted others. Wrapped in a figurative blanket of loneliness, the drunk is all alone among 100,000 spectators at a football game—if he or she is intoxicated. Loneliness is found in all sorts of strange places, such as in the hustle and bustle of a factory, or the false gaiety of a rowdy party.

But loneliness is not merely the state of being or feeling alone. It is the antithesis of solitude, with which many confuse it. The difference between the two is the difference that separates pain from joy. Loneliness involves hurting; within solitude is gratification. The one is an empty and frightening existence, the other a fulfilling consciousness.

Loneliness usually is thrust upon us. Solitude must be willingly and carefully sought. When we are lonely, if we can learn to enjoy our own company, we can convert the unwanted loneliness into rewarding solitude. Unless we escape our bondage with companionship with others or with meditation, chronic loneliness has the power to destroy.

Solitude can be productive in motivating character growth. In solitude, we have an opportunity to find, and know, ourselves. This awareness opens the door for improvement in attitudes and behavior. Those who argue that they cannot utilize solitude any more than they can loneliness usually are still emotionally immature.

Yet there is something more dangerous than loneliness itself. That is the *fear* of feeling lonely. This anticipation of discomfort and abandonment will devour all our defenses against loneliness long before we get there. When we act as though people won't want to be around us, they won't.

As alcoholics we relate our drinking problem to the "disease" of loneliness, because the victims of both usually suffer for years without recognizing or accepting the reality of what is wrong.

In the same manner, it is as difficult for us to tell others that we are powerless over alcohol as it is for those who suffer from loneliness to confess that they feel their inadequacy as human beings makes them unloved and unwanted.

Society places such a high premium on self-reliance that most persons would "rather die" than ask for help with a mental health problem or, above all, admit that they cannot cope with themselves. This is why alcoholics refuse to admit they cannot drink like others who can control their intake.

All loneliness is compounded by the lonely. Invariably, the person "in the dumps" will choose to listen to songs like "Born to Lose" and "I'll Never Smile Again" while feeling sorry for him- or herself.

The "rat race" of materialistic living tends to make anyone a loner. Everyday stresses direct us toward being introverted. Today's harvest of uncertainties leads even the most stable toward a feeling that mere survival is the most we can hope for.

We are told from childhood that the smart ones succeed independently. We envy those who make it entirely on their own. And it is natural that many who get to the top quickly and find they have attained all they ever wanted, descend into loneliness because they have no more interesting mountains to climb.

A fantasy world often beckons to those who have "been everywhere and done everything." This leads to an inability to communicate. It is not easy for us, who often have never needed anyone else before, to have room for others when we enter our lonely world.

All lonely people yearn to "get out of their bag." The search for exits can become obsessive. With obvious aggressiveness, some of us forced ourselves upon others. Naturally, we wanted assurance that we were worthy of friendship, loyalty, and love.

Such a drive, in itself, would not be fraught with trouble if, in wanting to "belong," we did not demand more of others than they were willing to give, or even capable of giving. But when what we received seemed inadequate, we were frustrated. Our feeling of rejection, of being "left out of life," sent us headlong back to loneliness.

Lonely people who can understand what they need and are capable of making realistic approaches to obtain a portion of their wants, are obviously not as likely to be stunned by disappointments. But many of us were incapable of this, and we headed straight for depression. We suffered long spells of insomnia, during which we pondered the fates that had drained pleasure from our lives. The most serious result was thoughts of suicide. In the grips of loneliness we drank to destroy ourselves.

Compulsiveness is the most popular way out for the lonely. Multitudes try to escape by excessive smoking, eating, sex, gambling, working and, of course, drinking. Some escape by running away. Some "run" by changing their lifestyles constantly—new friends, bars, jobs, neighborhoods, hobbies, lovers. Changing things was obsessive with us. We refer to these experiments as "geographics."

Researchers into loneliness agree that the first step in being free of this empty feeling is to show lonely people that they are surrounded by hosts of people as lonely as they are—people with whom to engage in mutual solutions.

Dr. John Milner of the University of Southern California School of Social Work told a writer recently that "what we need is some organization which is not segregated by age or sex or vices or addictions, such as Alcoholics Anonymous," where the lonely can benefit from one another through individual experiences, strengths, and hopes.

We've learned in recovery that, if we are lonely, to help ourselves we must go in the opposite direction of our loneliness—toward *people*. We have realized that we truly are people who need people and who *know* it. We can well recite: "*We* can do what *I* can't."

On our own, each of us can remind ourselves of some powerful, healing concepts: that gratitude is the aristocrat of emotions; that we must be honest with the wish to be honest; that a desire to have a desire for growth can achieve miracles; that there must be a willingness to be willing; and that a humble hope for humility will bring the wisdom to see things as God sees them for us.

■　■　■

Spiritual Living

The disease of alcoholism is so strongly addictive that few people can achieve a lasting recovery by concentrating only on physical, intellectual, and emotional areas of their lives. A more secure and lasting sobriety seems to result when we open our minds to the acceptance of spiritual living.

Contrary to popular belief, spiritual programs for recovering alcoholics are rarely religious in nature. Recovery programs stress the concept that the "spiritual" is simply the life force opposite of the physical being. The "spiritual" is actually a nonmaterial motivation for better living and for progress.

Maintaining sobriety requires much more than just keeping the plug firmly planted in the jug. Those of us who have experienced spiritual awakenings know that we must banish from our lives the emotional hang-ups and intellectualizing that endanger our sobriety.

Swiss psychologist Carl Jung noted that the Latin word *spiritus* means alcohol and that from this same root word comes the word *spiritual*. Of this irony Jung commented, "We use the same word root for the highest religious experience as we do for the most depraving poison."

In AA, those who suffer emotional stress are advised to "Let go and let God." It is important to note that this phrase does not encourage cowardly escapism. In fact, both persistence and diligence are needed to seek and accept divine guidance in today's world. The challenge is greater when society puts so much emphasis on the physical and the intellectual.

Recovering alcoholics believe that the key slogan "Let go and let God" means seeking to rid the mind of all doubts and fears about one person's capacity to make progress. In recovery, we reach for long-term gains in well-being instead of short-term pleasure. "Letting go" tends to make us ready for improvement.

When we "let go," we are expressing belief that we can approach spiritual living by three means—*love, service,* and *prayer/meditation.*

Recovering people sometimes compare sobriety attained through faith in a "Higher Power" with reaping the harvest from a fruit tree. Looking at things figuratively, prayer and meditation are the water and fertilizer; love is the vital sunshine; service is the pruning and the assorted tasks of harvesting. Of course, all three elements are required to reap a bumper crop.

Sober alcoholics believe in their hearts that spiritual contentment can be found as effectively by bending down to help someone stand again as by bending the knees in prayer. Service need be nothing more complicated than simply wishing others well; this change of attitude cannot help but inspire others and encourage character growth as well.

The fellowship of Alcoholics Anonymous would die without an active service component, for messages cannot carry themselves. But before anyone can perform a service, his or her own house must be "in order." This primary focus on self-improvement, of course, helps keep the alcoholic sober.

In letting God help us, we are essentially asking love to assume control of our actions. So long as we cling to

Spiritual Living 115

the right to reject or criticize, we are not equipped to turn a problem over for advice and help.

Many people maintain that most character defects are merely perversions of the love instinct and that these character defects thrive when love is absent. Those who love characteristically find it difficult to lie, cheat, and steal; those who love find it difficult to refuse opportunities to provide service.

There is a theory that alcoholism grows out of love starvation in people who are born with a great capacity for love. In recovery, these people may step from a fearful world into a world where they care enough for others that they are willing to labor long and hard to help other people rid themselves of their alcohol dependency.

"Letting go" should never be a cop-out on our responsibility to do the "footwork" necessary for our recovery programs and to help other addicted people. Even prayer must be a sincere act of love and service. We cannot ask for an ability or a reward that will give us an advantage over others. This kind of request is not "service."

We invariably pray only for the ability to cope with an active life. We are taught that action on our part must follow prayer. We are constantly told, "If you pray for potatoes, be sure to carry a spading fork." Sobriety must be worked for and prayed for as well.

■ ■ ■

Use of Prayer

When we were drinking compulsively, most of the praying we did probably took place as we were flat on our backs and moaning "God help me." At those times, most of us promised never to touch another drop of alcohol if God would just take us out of our agony and let us live. But it seems that once we were sober, we never remembered or admitted that we had prayed for help at all.

Yet the physical comfort and emotional serenity that developed and continued to grow after a period of sobriety seemed to cultivate in us enough gratitude to make us willing to pray for help in staying abstinent.

In recovery, we learn so much about the power of prayer. For example, we learn that while kneeling to pray is not necessary, it can help. We learn that arrogance is almost impossible for someone who is down on his or her knees. We learn that by heading off arrogance, we can open the door to humility—a quality that is absolutely necessary if we are to learn new things.

Even if we do not participate in the rituals of organized religion or do not believe in the importance of the church, it is vital to our recovery that we accept the concept of a power greater than ourselves.

Prayer helps us find four things: *faith*, *dedication* to a program of recovery, *knowledge* of how to achieve growth of character, and *strength* to cope with the challenges of life without resorting to the crutch of alcohol.

Without prayer and our resulting conscious contact with a power greater than ourselves, sobriety will be poised for a sudden, unexpected flight from our grasp. Why? It is difficult for *anyone* conversing with God to have time to conjure up the number one enemy of serenity and sobriety— resentment.

Those who stubbornly resist prayer are crying out that they're lost before they even can be rescued. In fact, when an alcoholic approaches sobriety with a desire to stop drinking, he or she is really saying an unconscious prayer. Prayer is sometimes no more than wanting something earnestly. When sobriety comes to people who want it earnestly, it is truly the *answer* to prayer.

Newcomers struggling with how to pray frequently are advised to make a good start by simply trying to find some good in people who they believe they dislike. Wishing someone well is prayer in its simplest form. Those of us who know the depths of alcoholic despair find that it is impossible to wish even our worst enemies another drink. Genuinely hoping for continued sobriety for all other alcoholics constitutes prayer.

Prayer is coupled with meditation in the AA Program. We are told that "Prayer is talking to God; meditation is listening for God's answers." The best kind of prayer, therefore, is a conversation between an individual and his or her Higher Power.

Hostile newcomers to the Program may be cautioned: "Instead of making prayer a monologue, as we arrogant ones do, try to stop now and then to listen." Another bit of solid advice to newcomers: "Prayer should never be carried out as around a bargaining table. Don't tell God that you will shape up if he makes something happen for you."

Perhaps the most difficult form of prayer for a skeptic or nonbeliever is the act of thanking a Higher Power for good things received. This kind of thanks cannot be given without humility. Some of us use an all-embracing prayer: "Thank you, God, for what you have given me, for what you have taken from me, and for what you have left me."

Alcoholics are notorious seekers of instant success: We want perfection overnight and we pile requests—one upon the other— until someone offers a caution: "You must not ask for more until you have become worthy of what you already have received."

We know there is an all-important step beyond prayer and meditation: putting them to use. This means action. We know that what we ask for while on our knees is not nearly as important as what we do about the answers once we are back on our feet.

■   ■   ■

The Sense of Belonging

Learning to feel "at home" is the most difficult adjustment we face as we seek help at an Alcoholics Anonymous meeting, at a session of group therapy, or in the chemical dependency treatment unit of an institution.

Identification with other alcoholics is not always easy, nor does the feeling of belonging with fellow sufferers always come quickly. Bewildered, we may hear hundreds of personal stories or bits of advice before we begin to share ourselves fully. That is why newcomers to AA are told to keep coming back in the following way: "Just bring the body, and the mind eventually will follow."

All kinds of people make up the multitude of alcoholics in this country. Many recovering alcoholics choose to say that "It takes what it takes to become an alcoholic and it takes what it takes to achieve sobriety." This is one way of saying that there is a wide variety of people who become alcoholic. And each alcoholic will reach a uniquely individual physical, mental, and emotional "bottom" through his or her own efforts. The same broad principle applies to the process of arresting the disease of alcoholism through total abstinence.

One man said this after his first AA meeting, "Wow! I never would have gotten *drunk* with those rummies, so why would I want to get *sober* with them?"

Millions of alcoholics have emerged from their first contacts with a group of recovering alcoholics, heads wagging and saying: "I never went that far. I never did what those bums did. I *can't* be an alcoholic." This kind of denial and conscious separation from other alcoholics is a familiar cry of those who seem to want to continue their behavior.

On the other hand, we frequently hear sober men and women report how they sat in shame and despair at their first meetings—feeling totally unworthy among smiling, happy, clean, sparkling-eyed people.

One woman, known affectionately as "the Duchess" by drunks in the skid row area she revisits now and then, relates that she felt unclean when she attended her first AA meeting asking for help: "I'd been kicked off skid row by the police because they said I was a bad influence on the other drunks who were trying to practice panhandling with honesty," she laughs. "I had no place to go, so I tried AA. The night I showed up, I had just recovered from delirium tremens. I looked at all those decent, respectable folks and was sure that if they ever found out what kind of person I was, they'd toss me out. Suddenly, I spotted three or four men who had been slobbering all over the corner of Fifth and Main only months before. I decided that if *they* were welcome in AA, *I* was, too."

Men and women without personal experience with alcoholism are inclined to generalize that "A drunk is a drunk." They seem not to realize that the causes of alcoholism are many and that those who suffer from its effects represent many different backgrounds and experiences.

Most nonalcoholics fail to realize the intensity of the physical pain and emotional anguish experienced by alcoholics. The common characterization of the alcoholic in the upper strata of society has been that of a fun-loving, irresponsible, childish person. This attitude results in a collective anger toward alcoholics who are then blasted by disciplined drinkers who may feel the need to judge and punish the alcoholic.

If it is not effective to punish with kindness, it is a practical solution to *release* with love. Those who cannot personally relate to the suffering of the alcoholic can serve the alcoholic best by turning him or her over to those who have admitted, dealt with, and conquered their own alcoholic pains.

This is how we come to feel such a sense of belonging in the program: Although we are all quite different, we share a history of pain. We understand one another in a way that outsiders cannot understand us. Even though some of us are sicker than others, we do not judge one another because we are all sick. And, for all of us, the solution to our problem is simply the same: don't drink and keep coming back.

It's a Simple Program

Stubbornly denying the fact that he could no longer control his drinking, a middle-aged man reluctantly attended an Alcoholics Anonymous meeting one night. Just as the meeting began, a young woman and her seven-year-old son sat down beside him. The man noticed that the young boy listened to the speakers at the meeting for about 10 minutes, then fell sound alseep.

When the meeting ended, the man gently jibed the boy asking, "What did you get out of the meeting, Sonny?" The youngster flashed a serious smile and said this: "You put the cork in your bottle and you don't ever, ever take it out again." Relating this story at an AA meeting years later, the man concluded: "I decided right then and there that if a seven-year-old kid could, in 10 minutes, grasp the secret of maintaining abstinence, I'd have to simplify my own attempts at recovery. And one of the ways I could simplify would be to let go of my demands to know the why and how of everything."

Recovering alcoholics like to say that traveling the road to sobriety is a simple journey for confused people with a complicated disease.

Once we are in recovery and find some security in our sobriety as well, many of us spend time studying the disease which we share with millions of people in this country. But during our last painful and frantic search for a way to stop drinking, we usually relied exclusively on the most simple of truths about fighting our addiction and compulsion. For example, when we asked how we got drunk, we may have been told this: "Simple. You took liquor into your mouth, then you swallowed it." That shouldn't be hard to comprehend but it *is*.

There are many miracles evident in the sustained sobriety of men and women once considered hopeless drunks. But, alas, there are no magical secrets in a program of recovery. One long-sober member of AA was approached by a newcomer to the fellowship who promptly offered the oldtimer a challenge: "Jack, remember you promised me that if I stayed away from booze for a week, you'd tell me the secret of this Program and why it works? The oldtimer nodded and said, "Our secret is that we just don't drink." After a week of abstinence, the newcomer understood the oldtimer and the power of that simple statement.

A newcomer quickly learns that the problem of the alcoholic is not to stop drinking; every alcoholic has stopped drinking a number of times . . . before he or she starts drinking to intoxication again. *The challenge is to not start again.* It is not the last drink that is responsible for a binge; it's the first drink that leads to the binge, because it stirs up a sleeping compulsion. Elementary reasoning? Yes, but it's a sad fact that many alcoholics who learn to live comfortably without alcohol often manage to complicate things for themselves. They complicate things by deducing that they have learned to "handle" alcohol again. Unfortunately, these folks may never get sober again, much less achieve sobriety.

How ironic that while we need simplicity in staying sober, we originally drank because of a complicated array of reasons. Indeed, every binge had its reasons for occurring. For example, some alcoholics were "weather boozers": If it was chilly, a drink for warmth was in order; if the day was hot, iced highballs would cool; dreary days called for the cheer that alcohol could deliver; a glorious day called for a spirited celebration to match the beauty. In recovery we come to know that nothing is bad or good enough to be *helped* by alcohol.

It is so very fortunate that the reach for sobriety is simple. Alcoholics have likely had their brains scrambled so much that it may be difficult for them to grasp anything complex or profound. But the one thing alcoholics really need to retain is this directive: *"Don't drink."* Furthermore, a drinking alcoholic tends to rationalize everything. Thankfully, analyzing is next to impossible during the early stages of recovery. Otherwise, the boozer would fantasize a dozen reasons why being sober won't work, then he or she would run for the bottle.

Fortunately, many of the alcohol-related losses (memory, judgment, reasoning power and capacity to learn) *can* be reversed. Unfortunately, however, alcohol addiction almost always leaves some permanent damage.

But, of course, *ongoing recovery* is not quite as simple as the number one sure-fire way to avoid alcohol: by saying "No," "No," and "No." Beyond this, reading, listening, meditating, and praying will tighten our grip on sobriety.

We call the Program simple because it relies on universal principles that are available to anyone at any time. As the saying goes: "Whenever there are two recovering alcoholics, there's a meeting." Furthermore, the program is based on simple honesty; we reclaim the reality of our past and recognize the simple fact that we cannot drink again. Simple, but not easy

People Who Need People

We recovering people learn that while no one else can achieve sobriety *for* us, we cannot accomplish sobriety alone. Alcoholics Anonymous was founded in 1935 by two "hopeless drunks" who discovered that despite their desire to be loners while drinking, alcoholics are, indeed, people who need people. And when our goal is recovery, we alcoholics need people more than ever.

We alcoholics are stubborn. We often protested that it was too frustrating to "talk up to" physicians, psychiatrists, clergymen, counselors, judges, or family members. We felt sure that these folks could not *possibly* know how much an alcoholic suffers while he or she is in the throes of withdrawal.

Medication, detoxification, or even hospitalization may have been our first need, but eventually we were directed to a contact with sober alcoholics.

Many alcoholics drink their way to such terribly low bottoms that they must find and hold fast to a faith that the uphill climb to a normal life is possible. When they are close to other recovering people, they have only to look around to get the message that "If those drunks can make it, so can I."

Mutual-help sessions served to restore us to membership in the human race. For too long a time, we had been forced to exist with what we felt was universal rejection. Life, for us, was a long series of doors slamming in our faces. When we were permitted to shed the role of outcast and find that nobody around us demanded to know why we were there, we could deal with our shame and let it go. We were finally free of the guilty feeling that we had been morally weak. We felt we belonged. It was such a relief to realize that people were no longer pointing at us in scorn.

We heard amusingly encouraging things such as: "Bring your body to our discussions, even if the mind stays outside. The brain will finally join you"; "Our suggestions ultimately will rub off on you"; "A man in a blue serge suit can't walk through a cotton field without picking up lots of fluff."

And we were particularly struck by the truth of another statement: "Even if you have doubts that you're an alcoholic, stick around. You can't possibly catch the disease from us."

The goal of people within such a group is, of course, to help bring us to a genuine acceptance of our disease. Each of us eventually had to grasp the awareness that we and all those around us had lost the ability to control our drinking. Our understanding that we are powerless over alcohol actually started us on our way to sobriety.

Only one status exists in an AA group—think of it as one straight line. In AA, there are no gurus to hand down dictums. Everyone in the Program knows that regardless of the period of successful abstention, each recovering person is exactly the same distance away from a binge—*one drink*. In AA, we exchange ideas for the same reason: to save a life. *Our own.*

While recovery must be a self-first effort, success does not come easily if the alcoholic attempts recovery in isolation. There is a vast difference between being "selfishly dry" and the sobriety practiced within a group. With group consciousness, "dryness" evolves into sobriety. Our goal as recovering people is to continue to *grow* in sobriety.

One of the primary deterrents in getting alcoholics to work with each other is the widely held belief that people become intoxicated because of weak will power. Many frightened addictive drinkers have been driven to feel that they must prove their personhood by displaying a strong will in subduing their "habit." But such personal resources seldom are enough to sustain recovery.

The sooner we realize that will power is useless in fighting alcoholism, the better. Knowing we have a disease is our first accomplishment. It then becomes obvious to us that people don't just resolve not to be sick. Will power is no defense for an attack of hay fever or hives when pollens are flying around us or we ingest the wrong foods.

Once we are welcomed by others into a recovery program, we experience a new existence. Our world of alcoholism was a lonely one, even when we were surrounded by those who loved us. In that "old world," our behavior was not understood. Now we need never be alone or misunderstood again.

The ability to share may come slowly because an entire lifetime of self-centeredness cannot be reversed with a snap of the fingers. But commitment strengthens when we realize that without individual participation, an AA group may die. And unless the group survives, the individual will be all alone once more.

■ ■ ■

Love

One of the greatest rewards of spiritual growth we experience in recovery is a new understanding of love. In the AA Fellowship, men and women of all ages and backgrounds become dependent on people who need people in order to live serenely and securely. Dr. Bob, one of the cofounders of Alcoholics Anonymous, told an assembly of members that the Twelve Steps reveal themselves in a mere two words—*love* and *service*. For some of us recovering people, this is the first time in our lives that we have found joy in caring and sharing with others.

Because of the all-out spirit of helping others that dominates the love between recovering people, we share both problems and solutions. This sharing is a wonderful example of what psychologists refer to as *mutuality*—the simple process of exchanging the gift of life. Mutuality makes it impossible to give without receiving and equally impossible to receive without giving.

Those of us who lived for years with the principle of "never bothering to help anyone who can't return the favor again and again," suddenly find in AA meetings that we are being told, "Let us love you until you can learn to love yourself."

Even the most reticent newcomer to a recovery group is likely to accept the broad definition of AA love as "wishing someone well." The newcomer may be told with a smile that this means that "you don't have to like the person you love." No recovering alcoholic would *ever* wish a fellow recovering person a return to the use of alcohol. To wish someone the best is to wish sobriety for him or her.

Early in recovery, we are advised to carry out at least one act of AA love daily without anyone knowing about it. Doing this has the effect of enhancing the learning of humility. And because humility ultimately means being teachable, it is a vital part of recovery. Humility also leads to gratitude, willingness, and honesty.

Early in sobriety, we may hear this: "It is easy to love lovable people. If you would experience the best of love, select someone who seems unlovable and direct your love at him or her until, in your mind, that person becomes lovable." When we learn to do this successfully, we reduce our tendency to be resentful.

Love is the force that makes any newcomer to a recovery program feel that he or she belongs. He or she discovers that there are no strangers in the AA fellowship—only new friends we have not yet met and loved.

In sobriety, we begin to understand both fellowship and friendship. We come to know forgiveness of others and forgiveness of ourselves. One of the most noticeable indications of love is the "welcome back" greeting, with open arms, for a member who has gone out into the world of drinking, then returned to AA for another try at complete and joyous sobriety. In any other realm of society, a rule breaker (the only rule in sobriety is "don't drink") is usually criticized, chastened, lectured to, punished, penalized, or even fined or jailed. *In AA, love embraces forgiveness.*

Love is the creative force that brings helpful emotions into use; love is also the result of freely choosing attitudes and actions that promote spiritual growth.

Love is the foundation for friendship and fellowship. It joins hands with good will, tolerance, happiness, patience, spirituality, and compassion. Love serves to remind us that success can never be demanded, only deserved.

Love is the motivation for persistence in carrying the message of hope to those who suffer. We serve with a principle from the Sermon on the Mount—"Go a second mile." Alcoholics who help other alcoholics go beyond the point where failure seems certain. They never give up. Second efforts, even third, fourth, and more efforts are sustained. Going to great lengths overrides the most common deterrents: obstinence, denials, rebuffs, and resistance. Love is the basis for believing and feeling that if one life can be changed, the giver-of-hope has not lived in vain.

The love of giving builds a desire for wisdom and a desire for the truths that can be carried to others. It is love that makes recovering alcoholics good listeners.

To a sober alcoholic, love has many definitions: being available to all who need comfort and advice; ability to relate to those suffering and those with problems; a desire to love one's fellow man.

Giving love requires that we travel a one-way street, that we give freely without demanding something in return. It is more important to give love than to be loved. The word itself is best used as a verb; love is active rather than passive or receptive.

To give love is to return to the world a precious gift that the giver borrowed at a time when he or she was desperately in need of support.